Many Mansions

Many Mansions

A Christian's Encounter with Other Faiths

With a new Introduction

Harvey Cox

Beacon Press Boston

Beacon Press
25 Beacon Street
Boston, Massachusetts 02108-2892

Beacon Press books
are published under the auspices of
the Unitarian Universalist Association
of Congregations.

99 98 97 96 95 94 93 92 8 7 6 5 4 3 2 1

Text design by Gwen Frankfeldt

Library of Congress Cataloging-in-Publication Data

Cox, Harvey Gallagher.
Many mansions : a Christian's encounter with other faiths : with a new introduction / Harvey Cox.
p. cm.
Includes bibliographical references.
ISBN 0-8070-1213-0 (pbk.)
1. Christianity and other religions. 2. Cox, Harvey Gallagher.
I. Title.
BR127.C66 1992
261.2–dc20 91-28603

*In my Father's house are many mansions:
if it were not so, I would have told you.*

John 14:2

Contents

Acknowledgments ix

Introduction to the Second Edition xi

1 Introduction: Jesus and Dialogue 1

2 The Gospel and the Koran 20

3 Christ and Krishna 45

4 Buddhists and Christians 74

5 Rabbi Yeshua ben Joseph 96

6 The Search for a Soviet Christ 125

7 Beyond Dialogue: Liberation Theology and Religious Pluralism 162

8 "The Heart of a Heartless World": Christians and Marxists Examine Religion 180

9 The Future of Religion 195

Bibliography 213

Acknowledgments

Most of the material in *Many Mansions* appears here for the first time in print. Earlier versions of some portions, however, have previously appeared elsewhere. Chapter 2 includes most of an article I published in *The Atlantic* in January 1981 entitled "Understanding Islam." Chapter 4 includes some material from my book *Turning East,* first published by Simon and Schuster in 1977. Chapter 7 represents a rewriting of some parts of my *Religion in the Secular City,* published by Simon and Schuster in 1985. Chapter 8 includes some pages from an article called "The Heart of a Heartless World," which I published in *Essays in Arts and Sciences* in May 1983. Finally, my concluding chapter is drawn from an essay that first appeared in a volume edited by Alberto Villoldo and Ken Dychtwald entitled *Millennium: Glimpses into the Twenty-first Century,* published by Houghton Mifflin in 1981. I am grateful to all my previous publishers for their permission to rewrite, retract, and reprint my previous thoughts. I would also like to thank my secretary, Margaret Studier, and my research assistant, David Melton, for the help they have given me with this book.

Introduction to the Second Edition

To his security guards the well-dressed woman who approached Rajiv Gandhi in the village of Sriperumbudur during the last days of his hard-fought electoral campaign in May 1991 appeared to be no different from the thousands of others who pushed close to touch his feet in a gesture of respect and veneration. In the Hindu tradition holiness is closely related to power, and was not this man—though currently out of high office—the last survivor of the once mighty dynasty begun with Jawaharlal Nehru, the associate of the Mahatma himself? And was he not the son of the martyred Indira, the dust of whose footsteps the faithful had sometimes scooped up to carry home as a source of blessing?

But this woman was no devotee. She belonged to a suicide squad drawn from a Sri Lankan separatist group called the Liberation Tigers of Tamil Eelam; and around her waist she carried a bomb that in a blinding orange blast destroyed herself, Rajiv Gandhi, and fifteen other people. The bomb was wired to explode just as she bowed in reverence.

Religious fanatacism, political violence, ethnic strife, communal hatred—all seemed to collide on that hot afternoon in Sriperumbudur. At the start of the 1990s on the subcontinent of India, which had once been regarded by many Westerners—perhaps with too much wishful thinking—as a world treasure house of spirituality and nonviolence, self-destruction seemed to be mounting. Earlier, in 1948, Mahatma Gandhi had been gunned down on his way to evening prayers. The assassin, a fellow Hindu, has been described as either enraged by the Mahatma's openness to Muslims or fearful that his suspicion of industrial development would prevent India from progressing. Nehru, while unquestionably devoted to Gandhiji, also feared that the deep-dyed religiosity of India was an albatross dragging India down. Even though he kept this sentiment mostly to himself, once at the dedication of a dam he angrily refused a garland of flowers from a local holy man muttering that this was just what India had to leave behind. Then Indira Gandhi died a victim of religious fury as well, slain by the Sikhs who were part of her own body guard, presumably in revenge for her ordering an attack on their Golden Temple at Amritsar.

At the moment the Tamil Tigers' bomb blew Rajiv to shreds, he was fighting what seemed to be a losing three-way electoral battle. His own Congress Party—tired and corrupt after decades of power—was opposed by both a secularizing coalition and the Bharativa Janata, a Hindu nationalist party, which for the first time since independence had pushed explicitly religious issues into the campaign. Over eight hundred people were killed in election-related incidents. There were many who seriously wondered whether India would survive. Was the Mahatma's dream of an era of respect and harmony among the country's various spiritual traditions only that, a chimera now evaporating in the blazing sun of Bharat? Would

India eventually explode into fragments like the body of Rajiv Gandhi, so disfigured and dismembered his corpse had to be immolated in a closed coffin?

India is not alone in its distress, however. Though its religious rivalries seem more lurid, India only represents a somewhat more fevered version of a distemper that affects most of the world. Since the publication of *Many Mansions* in 1989 much has happened to demonstrate the pressing urgency of deepened interfaith communication. In addition to the assassination of Rajiv Gandhi, two other occurrences further dramatize the desperate need for such dialogue. The first is the crumbling of communism in Eastern Europe, and the maelstrom of old enmities loosed in the process. The second is the Gulf War with its ominous undertones of what the French press at the time referred to as the *guerre des cultures*. These all thrust to the fore the continuing animosities that still persist among and within the spiritual traditions of the world.

Lifting the lid of Soviet tyranny from the nations behind what used to be called the iron curtain sparked a brief moment of euphoria as exultant people sang in Prague's Wenceslas Square and danced to rock and roll music on the punctured wall at the old Fredrichsstrasse crossing point in Berlin. But the music had hardly faded before the shrieks and accusations of old animosities began. Jubilation turned into rancor. Ethnic tensions, often abetted by ancient religious divisions, broke out like plagues that had lain dormant in the sewers awaiting their moment to pounce.

In Roman Catholic Poland it was anti-Semitism. Ugly graffitti of a Star of David hanging on a gallows appeared scrawled on walls in Warsaw and Cracow. This in a country where the Nazi trains to Auschwitz had rumbled undisturbed by the local populace, where now only a tiny remnant of the thriving prewar Jewish community survived. It was not at all clear that Pope John Paul II's heartfelt pleas to his fellow Slavs against anti-Semitism, made during his triumphal tour of Poland in June 1991, had helped. Instead, his message caused new ill feelings. In one of his homilies the pope compared abortion—a vexed political issue in Poland—to the Nazi Holocaust. Many Jewish leaders and others were enraged by the analogy. Some called his remarks thoughtless and outrageously superficial. French Jews called them pernicious, incompetent, and unacceptable. But at Olsztyn, Poland, a Vatican spokesman said there was nothing wrong in the comparison, that both abortion and the Holocaust represent "great attacks on life in this century."

The exchange was a stalemate, but it demonstrated that Christians of all denominations need to prepare themselves much better if they are to enter with genuine seriousness and sensitivity into the dialogue with Jews that the pope himself has commended. This interfaith dialogue is clearly needed. A recent poll found that 40 percent of Poles and 23 percent of Czechs do not want a Jew as a neighbor. In Russia, where hundreds of Orthodox churches have been reopened, a rancid anti-Semitism has also reemerged, with some Russians blaming everything from Stalin's crimes to the current butter shortage on the Jews. No wonder so many thousands of Soviet Jews are fleeing to Israel where their arrival in great numbers has added fuel to another religious and ethnic hot spot by taking away jobs that were once held by Palestinian Muslims.

Old wounds heal slowly. No one who glances at the map of Yugoslavia can fail to notice that the borders dividing the two republics now seeking their independence from the rest of the country—Slovenia and Croatia—run along the historic fault line between the millennia-old Roman Catholic and Orthodox realms. And in Romania, it was the pastor of a small, minority Hungarian Protestant community in Timişoara who catalyzed the rebellion against the Ceausescu regime, in part as a struggle for religious liberty. Yet, as the people took to the streets, the leaders of the Romanian Orthodox church remained relatively quiescent, perhaps fearful of losing the church's privileged position with the government. They later apologized for their inaction.

In Leipzig, in what was once East Germany, the postwall battle focuses more on values. Church leaders who helped guide and nurture the remarkable nonviolent revolution against communist rule—sometimes by reading to the people from the books of Martin Luther King before they marched—notice that as consumer goods and gadgets begin to stream in, the longest queues form at the porno movies and sex shops. Ironically, in that same city the young people who carry placards and demonstrate most energetically against the "porn wave" are shaven-headed neo-Nazis wearing leather jackets and swastika medallions. In short, the immediate result of the liberation of Europe seems not to be an unequivocal step toward democracy and decency but an almost instant reversion to the seething religious animosities and cultural divisions of the past. For anyone who remembers the "brown decade" before World War II, the events of the past two years in Europe cannot help but inspire a chilling sense of *déja vu.*

When the Gulf War began in January 1991, France—the European nation with perhaps the longest and most complex relations with the Muslim world—was torn asunder by a debate over the war's religious and cultural meaning. Was it a *guerre des cultures,* pitting the democratic, "Christian" civilization of the West against Islamic society? Or was it something else? The participation of most of the Arab states on the allied side seemed at first to confuse the debate since Saddam Hussein, despite his prayer rug posturing, was widely perceived to be anti-Muslim. But the question persisted. Some French writers, alarmed by the growing power of Muslim fundamentalist groups such as the Islamic Salvation Front in Algeria and the Renaissance Party in Tunisia—countries with which France has had a long and turbulent history—contended that the root cause of the war was the failed Western effort to foster economic development, with its inevitable effect on values, in the Arab world. As in Iran, they argued, such aborted development (and there were grounds to believe it would always be aborted) inevitably produces a fundamentalist reaction. Faced with the cruel choice "between Mecca and mechanization," they held that the Arab masses will finally choose Mecca and will lash out against those they believe have defaced the family and societal values enshrined in the Koran.

This is a troubling analysis. Was the Gulf War a resumption of the millennial struggle that began with the sweep of the Prophet's bands across Northern Africa and into Spain and Sicily in the seventh century, then continued with the Crusades, and now has lain dormant during the present period of fading Western colonial hegemony? Was it yet another battle between radically disparate societies rooted in fundamentally different religious worldviews? Was this—not oil, or the rights of small nations—what the war was about? The strenuous effort of Pope John Paul II to revive the notion of a "Christian Europe" stretching, as Charles de Gaulle used to put it, "from the Atlantic to the Urals," has lent a certain credibility to the idea.

But for the millions of Muslims who are citizens of France, and for the other millions of their faith who live permanently in London, Hamburg, Milan, and hundreds of other cities in allegedly "Christian" Europe, such a definition of Desert Storm has not brought much comfort. Nor has it appealed to the increasingly articulate community of Muslim scholars and intellectuals who live either in the West or who—from Beirut or Cairo—participate in Western political and philosophical debates. One such scholar is Daryush Shayegan, whose remarkable book *Qu'est-ce qu'une Révolution Religieuse?* (*What Is a Religious Revolution?*) has already set the stage for the *guerre des cultures* argument. Shayegan concedes that some Muslim thinkers regard democracy as the equivalent of unbelief, a historical monstrosity from which it is now time to make an unequivocal break. But he believes such a break will never happen, in part because Islam itself imbues people with a functional equivalent of the Protestant ethic. Like Puritanism, even though it can appear fanatic Islam teaches equality, respect for others, and hard work. It will inevitably create the kind of culture in which democracy will develop.

Shayegan's is not a lone voice. Other Muslim scholars argue that religious tolerance is rooted in the Koran and that the "Cadillac sheiks" of the oil emirates are cynically misusing Islam to prop up their unpopular governments. Some call for a Muslim liberation theology which might help the Arab peoples draw on the Koran to escape from their current victimization at the hands of their own elites. Perhaps in that way, they contend, the painful blurring of Muslim identity that Salman Rushdie chronicles so pungently in *Satanic Verses*—neither truly "modern," and not wanting to be, nor really "traditional," and not wanting to be—could be overcome and an authentically Arab or even Muslim form of democracy, quite different from that of the West, could be born.

Is this a genuine possibility? I think it is. But if a democratic future can come to Islamic countries it will depend on at least two critical factors. One is the experience of those millions of Muslims who now live in diaspora in the West.

The other is a resolution of the seemingly intractable conflict between the Jewish state of Israel and the Muslim nations. Both factors dramatize the desperate need for serious and patient interreligious dialogue.

Let's look at the Islamic diaspora. How will Muslims from the Middle East who currently live in Liverpool or Ann Arbor or Dallas actually experience the West, given all the contradictory labels their teachers have attached to it, as the land of fabulous opportunity and the great devil, as the pinnacle of modernity and the abyss of debauchery? How will they experience Christians and Jews, whom their mentors variously designate as "peoples of the book" whose faith is to be respected, as infidels, or as polytheists? Much of the answer to this question depends on the attitudes of Western Jews and Christians toward the Muslims in our midst. Will we continue to regard them—as many of us now do—as bigots and fanatics, ever ready to stone adulterous couples and to lop off the hands of thieves? Or will we, like thousands of small, grassroots Christian and Jewish congregations already do, open our doors to help them, welcome them, and learn about their faith?

Everywhere I go I am impressed both by the scale of the task and by the imaginative way so many Christians, Jews, and Muslims are addressing it. In Milan, Catholic parishes are assisting Muslim newcomers to find housing and employment, and the bishop has discouraged any effort to proselytize them. In London, where as many as 70 percent of the children in some school districts are Muslims, British teachers have introduced courses on the Koran and the history of Islam. In Massachusetts, a young Jewish woman has organized a highly successful dialogue group for Jewish, Christian, and Muslim women. In San Diego, the council of churches cooperates with local mosques in sponsoring interfaith potluck dinner and conversation evenings. In some American cities, councils of churches, which only recently opened their ranks to synagogues, are beginning to welcome mosques. One hears more frequently now the phrase "Jewish-Christian-Muslim tradition."

The stakes in all this are very high. If the young Muslims who come to study at MIT and Cal Tech, and the millions who have settled here and whose children will grow up in the West, have a positive experience of democracy and religious pluralism, they will inevitably wield some positive influence on thinking and policy about these issues in the Islamic heartland. Yet if they encounter rejection, suspicion, and ignorant stereotyping, they will just as surely slide toward the very Islamic fundamentalism their most thoughtful leaders want to avoid.

As for the Jewish-Muslim dialogue, it is rendered more complex of course—much more complex—by the close bond that ties the world Jewish community in diaspora to the Jewish state of Israel. The complexity has many layers. There is a sense in which Israel is the "other" against which much of the current Islamic revival has come into being. Here Israel seems to pose a double threat. It is both a religious non-Muslim state in an area of increasingly self-conscious Muslim renascence and a prime example of successful economic development, the modernization many Muslims both want and fear with what is often a highly intense ambivalence.

On the Jewish side, dialogue is made more difficult by the deep divisions within the world Jewish community (especially within the large segment of Jewry that resides in America); by the resentment Conservative and Reformed Jews feel toward the power of the Orthodox rabbinate in Israel; by the cleft between religious and nonreligious Jews; and by the polemic between Jewish hawks and Jewish doves in and outside Israel (with the "religious" parties usually on the hawkish side). None of this is helped by the curious alliance that has sprung up between right-wing Jews who want to rebuild the temple and American Protestant fundamentalists who seek to hurry Christ's second coming; nor by the growing strength of the Gush Emunim, a religious party that believes God wants Israel to encompass all of Palestine.

The situation is hardly a promising one for dialogue. Indeed the incident in 1990 when Israeli soldiers near the Great Mosque of Jerusalem fired on Muslim demonstrators, who had thrown stones at Jews praying at the Wailing Wall, illustrates just how close the raw edges are. Still, despite all the difficulties and obstacles, some courageous Jews, Muslims, and even Christians continue to defy pressures; they meet, converse, and try to find a way out of the morass. But here again the example of what happens in the diaspora is critical. If the three Abrahamic faiths can learn to listen to one another's stories in Europe and America—and there is some evidence that they can—this is bound to have a positive effect in the Middle East.

There will never be peace in the world, it has been said, until there is peace among the religions. The statement seems undeniably true to me, and therefore the saga of personal encounters with people of other faiths that I unfold in *Many Mansions,* both the victories and breakthroughs and the frustrations and disappointments, seems ever more pertinent. I write as a Christian, advocating not tolerance, which though a useful virtue is hardly enough today, but something more demanding. We who try to follow the Prince of Peace should be actively trying to weave networks of trust and reconciliation among the faiths wherever we can. We should be doing this not just to promote some vague broad-mindedness but because the One who instructed us to seek first the Reign of God requires it.

Walls go up and walls come down. I lived in Berlin just after its monstrosity of masonry and razor wire went up, and I am grateful that I lived to see its collapse. Must war return incessantly to our race despite our best efforts to banish it? And will assassinations and murders never cease? Today the world is too small and too mightily armed to allow these ingrained bad habits to run their course. And it is far too small to afford the luxury of religious xenophobia. Interfaith dialogue is interlaced with stubborn political, tribal, gender, and racial distrust, which gives us all the more reason to learn, not in theory but in actual practice, how to reach across the confessional chasms that separate us to find common ground. This is what *Many Mansions* tries, not always successfully but—I hope—persistently, to do.

Harvey Cox
South Strafford, Vermont
July 1991

Many Mansions

1

Introduction: Jesus and Dialogue

Has the great dialogue among the world religions stalled, the dialogue that so many of us welcomed so warmly and so recently? Why has the "wider ecumenism," which had offered hope of crossing not only denominational but faith lines as well, begun to sputter and stammer and, in many instances, simply to stop? Why have relations among the ancient spiritual traditions of the human family, which many of us believed were improving a few years back, turned rancorous and even violent as new outbreaks of separatism, xenophobia, and hostility erupt?

To make matters worse, these same faith communities are increasingly divided within themselves, and the rifts are often exacerbated by political tensions. Sunni and Shiite Muslims declare each other to be worse than infidels. Jews, both pious and secular, who want to find some way to live at peace with Palestinians, despair over the zealotry of the Gush Enumin, who believe God has given their people land on which Palestinians have dwelt for generations. Christians who work for interfaith understanding have been shocked and perplexed by the attacks of fundamentalists who condemn them as traitors to the Gospel but who themselves seem willing to cooperate with those heathen if their politics are acceptable. Indeed, people in any religious tradition who are committed to dialogue often find themselves upbraided as turncoats by their own brothers and sisters.

Admittedly, the picture is not unrelievedly gloomy. Here and there, small circles of Muslims and Jews, Hindus and Sikhs, Buddhists and Christians, continue to meet and talk and even to work together, but they do so despite the currents that seem to be flowing against them. What has gone wrong?

I believe that the most nettlesome dilemma hindering interreligious dialogue is the very ancient one of how to balance the universal and the particular. Every world faith has both. Each nourishes in rite and saga its own unique and highly particular vision. Maybe it is the message of the one true God delivered without blemish to the Prophet. Or it is the fathomless Brahman from which all that is and all that is not come and return. Or the faithful Son of God dying on the cross. Or the supreme moment when enlightenment comes to the patient figure seated under the Bo tree. Or the bestowal of the life-giving gift of Torah on a chosen people. Whatever it is, the particular hub defines the center around which each world faith rotates, endowing it season after season and century after century with its characteristic ethos.

At the same time every world faith, if it is truly a world faith and not a local cultus, also generates a universal vision. Brahman embraces all ages, each drop of water, and every savior. The Koran names a God who created all people equal and who decrees that a unified human family should mirror his sublime unity. The dying Christ is raised to life by a God who favors the outcasts and the heartbroken and who summons all tribes and tongues into an inclusive community of service and praise. The bodhisattva compassionately refuses to enter nirvana until every sentient being can enter with him.

Thus each world faith has both its axis and its spokes, its sharply etched focus and its ambient circumference. Further, it is the mark of a truly world faith that these two dimensions are not only held together: they strengthen and reinforce each other. Somewhere, somehow, all that now seems fragmented and contradictory, all that appears tragic or inexplicable, is gathered into a single mystery of meaning and value.

The crisis in the current state of interfaith dialogue can be stated simply: the universal and the particular poles have come unhinged. Faced with a world in which some form of encounter with other faiths can no longer be avoided, the ancient religious traditions are breaking into increasingly bitter wings. Those who glimpse the universal dimension advocate dialogue and mutuality. They search out what is common and that which unites. Those who emphasize the particular often shun dialogue and excoriate their fellow believers who engage in it more fiercely than they condemn outsiders. This ugly chasm, running through all religions, gives rise to a "worst-possible" scenario one might envision if the current trend persists. Imagine a time when tiny cadres of "dialoguers" would perch on the fringe of each faith community, endlessly refining the language and concepts in which they converse with those on the universalist wings of the other faiths. Meanwhile, on the opposite side in each religion, zealous cohorts of radical particularists would congregate, anathematizing their backsliding coreligionists for compromising the truth by fraternizing with the reprobate. It is not an attractive prospect.

But we need both poles. I count myself as one of the universalists. Yet sometimes as I have sat in genteel—or even mildly acrimonious—gatherings of urbane representatives of different faith traditions, under the auspices of the World Council of Churches or the Center for the Study of World Religions at Harvard, my mind has strayed from the conference room out to those jagged corners of the world where other confessors of these same faiths are killing or proselytizing—or just frigidly ignoring—each other. I have wondered at such moments whether the "dialogue" has not become a tedious exercise in preaching to the converted and I have secretly wished to bring some of those enthusiasts in. Deprived of the energy such particularists embody, a dialogue-among-the-urbane can, and sometimes does, deteriorate into a repetitious exchange of vacuities. It could end with a whimper.

At the same time I fully believe that without the large-hearted vision of the universal that the interfaith conversation incarnates, particularism can deteriorate into fanaticism. And in our present overarmed world, zealotry can easily hasten the moment when everything ends with a bang. So we are left with a paradox. Without the universal pole, there would be no dialogue at all. But without the particular, the dialogue dissipates its source of primal energy. Without the Cross or the Koran or the Bo tree, the religions that were called into being by these sacred realities would atrophy and along with them the inclusive visions they spawned would fade away too. The paradox of the great world faiths is that they both create a dream of a single human family and threaten that dream at the same time. What can be done?

It seems too formulaic simply to say that the universalists and the particularists need each other, especially since they seldom think they do. Still, I believe they do, and as one who has participated in the dialogue for decades, I propose—in this book—to draw on my own experience to show how the indispensable element of particularity can be brought back in. To do so, however, will require me to point out, as I begin, the two most salient ways in which Christians who engage in the dialogue have—often quite inadvertently—neglected the hub in their commendable effort to enlarge the rim.

The first way the particular is diminished in interfaith dialogue is through the loss of the personal voice. Dialogue often climbs quickly to airy exchanges about "Christianity" and "Buddhism" or one of the other faiths. The dialoguers, who are frequently trained to think in abstract, conceptual terms, are sometimes reluctant to say much about "my" faith in Jesus Christ, or "my" devotion to Krishna, or "my" path toward enlightenment. Even the language of "our" faith or "our" path is often left behind as the talk soars into that realm of discourse (invaluable for its own purposes) one finds in an academic seminar on comparative religion. Soon people are yawning and glancing at their watches.

I believe a certain careful and modest restoration of personal narrative—call it "testimony" if you will—can help restore some of the life-giving particularity to the dialogue among religions. After all, it is never the religions themselves that converse but individual people who embody those religions. I have seen more than one interfaith colloquium that was drifting toward death by tedium restored to life when someone had the courage to speak personally rather than in general terms. For this reason, the essays in this book grow almost entirely from my own encounters with actual people of other faiths—enriched and broadened of course by reading and reflection.They are unified by the lived experience of one person. *Many Mansions* is not about "the" Christian dialogue with other religions but about one Christian's encounters with particular people of other faiths.

The second way Christian participation in the dialogue has sometimes lost sight of the particularity pole has been by soft-pedaling the figure of Jesus himself. There are many exceptions to this sotto voce treatment of Christ. Still, I have noticed—as will become evident later on—that when reference to Jesus is postponed or downplayed, conversations between Christians and people of other traditions tend to become arid, but when the figure of Jesus is brought to the fore, either by the Christians or—as sometimes happens—by the others, the dialogue comes alive.

One can of course understand why Christians who believe in the dialogue do not want to push Jesus down other people's throats as soon as the opening gavel has been rapped. After all, Jesus is in some ways the *most* particularistic element of Christianity, and in an interreligious dialogue one is presumably trying—at least at first—to present the less divisive aspects of one's own tradition. The trouble is that, not only has this understandable reticence deprived the dialogue of the vigor it needs to survive, but it has also produced another unfortunate consequence. This secondary result is that Christians who think of Jesus as a model in other areas of their lives do not look to his example or teaching for direction in the dialogue itself. I think this twofold neglect of the figure of Jesus—both as a theme and as a source of guidance—has exacted a heavy toll.

I do not mean to suggest that those Christians who even now are working with great dedication in talks with Buddhists or Muslims or Jews never mention Christology (that branch of Christian theology that deals with the meaning of Jesus Christ). They do. Often they seek to find some bridge to the other faiths through a "cosmic Christ" such as the one portrayed in the Epistle to the Ephesians, a Christ who is said to be present throughout the universe and therefore presumably can be also found in the lived worlds of Hindus and Muslims. More frequently, however, the Christian participants have tried to base the dialogue on completely different facets of religious tradition. Sometimes, for example, they turn to the idea of God the Creator, the Mystery out of whom all that is emerges. At other times, they focus on the Divine Spirit, present in every person or even in every sentient being. In recent decades, they have preferred to explore the experience of faith itself as a universal human experience that exhibits common stages of development through the succeeding phases of human life. Most recently, they have sought to wrestle—together with people of other faiths—with the awful issues everyone must confront today—nuclear war, hunger, disease, the despoiling of the ecosphere—and to reach into the various traditions as possible sources of values and visions for facing such horrors. These paths to interfaith encounter differ markedly, but they all have one thing in common: they keep the historical Jesus of the Gospels distinctly in the background.

Each of these approaches to the crafting of an adequate Christian grasp of the multiplicity of faiths has its value. Each has advanced the dialogue in some measure. We need to continue to try to work with all of them. Still, I confess that I find these approaches, all of which hold the Jesus-fact in abeyance, not wholly satisfactory. The problem with them is twofold. First, for the vast majority of Christians, including those most energetically engaged in dialogue, Jesus is not merely a background figure. He is central to Christian faith. Not only do the Christian dialoguers recognize this, but so do their Muslim, Buddhist, Shinto, Hindu, and Jewish conversation partners. Wherever one starts, whether with creation (which, incidentally, is not a particularly good place to begin a dialogue with Buddhists, who reject the whole notion), with the omnipresent enlivening Spirit, with the faith experience as such, or with something else, any honest dialogue between Christians and others will sooner or later—

and in my experience it is usually sooner—have to deal with the figure of Jesus.

Yes, some might say, but is it not better to delay so potentially divisive a topic until some more inclusive groundwork has been laid? This may be the case in some instances, but I have never been persuaded that an interfaith dialogue is enhanced by designing it like one of those elementary collections for teaching the piano that begins with "Frère Jacques" and works up to Chopin preludes at the end. Everyone always knows that the question of who Jesus was and is, and what he means today, will inevitably appear. Until it does, it sometimes feels as though one is—at least to some degree—engaging in the necessary pleasantries that often precede a genuine conversation but are really not integral to it. When will the other shoe drop?

The second part of my problem with dialogue tactics that play down the Jesus factor is that—surprisingly—it is just this factor that the non-Christian participants often seem most interested in and most eager to get to. This is not something one is led to expect will happen in interfaith dialogue. But it does. Indeed, it happens so often that it raises serious questions about the other approaches, at least insofar as they try to proceed—ever so carefully and judiciously, they suppose—without this central point up front.

It took me a lot of time and many false starts to learn this. I too wanted to minimize the possibility of giving needless offense to the people of other faiths who had taken the venturesome step of entering into dialogue with me: to steer clear of unnecessary roadblocks or any suggestion of proselytizing. But I kept discovering that my tactics for nurturing the tender shoot of interfaith exchange did not connect with those of my partners across the table. I too tried to avoid talking about Jesus too quickly, but I soon discovered my interlocutors wanted me to, and their bearing sometimes suggested that they did not believe they were really engaged in a brass-tacks conversation with a Christian until that happened. Of course in this respect they were right.

The "others" want to hear what Christians think about Jesus. When Chogyam Trungpa, a Tibetan lama, invited me to teach summer school at the Naropa Institute in Boulder, Colorado, the first Buddhist higher educational institution in the United States, I accepted. I then suggested several alternative topics for my lectures and seminars, all leaning toward a comparative approach to religion. Trungpa and his fellow Buddhists were not interested. Instead, the course they encouraged me to offer was "The Life and Teachings of Jesus." A few years later, when I had my first serious conversation with a Muslim, he immediately wanted to compare Jesus with the prophet Muhammad. Shortly afterward, when I was asked to address a gathering of Vaishnava Hindu scholars during a trip to India, I carefully chose a safe "universal" topic—I think it was something like "the role of religion in the modern world." The Indian teachers sat patiently through my presentation and the long translation that followed. But, when the discussion period came, the first question they asked me was what I believed about Jesus and the form of love he exhibited (*agapē*). Soon we were all talking about Jesus, and then about the love Krishna shows to a devotee and the devotee to Krishna. My efforts at theological prudence, going slow, avoiding possibly thorny issues—although I certainly meant well—had merely succeeded in delaying the real exchange for two hours. I came away convinced that, whatever might be said for the other modes of dialogue, in my own future opportunities I would not assume that my partners wanted me to hold the Jesus factor in abeyance. More recently, other Christians who have engaged in difficult but real dialogue have come to the same conclusion. The only person I know who has ever met the Ayatollah Khomeini told me that the first thing Khomeini wanted to talk about was Jesus.

Of course, merely suggesting that Jesus be made more central to the dialogue does not solve anything at all. The questions of *what* role Jesus plays and *how* he is introduced still persist. This is why I have always been so intrigued by the "many mansions" Jesus speaks of in John 14:2, which I quoted at the beginning of this book, as well as by John 14:6: "I am the way, the truth, and the life: no man cometh unto the Father, but by me." These verses stand only a few lines away from each other in the same chapter of the same Gospel. But they have traditionally supplied both the dialogic universalists and the antidialogic particularists with their favorite proof texts. Those who look with appreciation on other faiths frequently cite John 14:2 and suggest that the "many mansions" may refer to the heavenly palaces in which Hindus and Buddhists will dwell—alongside Christians—in the hereafter. Those who insist that all others must accept Christ or be damned, however, prefer to cite John 14:6 and declare that Jesus alone is the one true way to salvation. What can we say about this curious juxtaposition of seemingly contradictory texts? Could it be telling us about the need to hold the universal and the particular together and about the central place Jesus must have for Christians even in the most expansive interfaith dialogue? The thoughts and experiences recounted in this book document my continuing struggle with these questions. I present them, not as a formula for all future dialogue, but as an addition and a complement to approaches I have found only partially satisfying. Thus my first point has been that, to place the figure of Jesus on the agenda of interfaith dialogue, far from killing it, actually enlivens it. My second point is related but different. It is that Jesus does have something vital to teach us about how to participate in interfaith dialogue. At first this may sound quite improbable. So far as we know, the rabbi from Nazareth never met a Buddhist or a Hindu. Islam did not appear until 600 years after his crucifixion. Despite speculations that regularly appear about his "hidden years," probably Jesus' interreligious experience was confined to the different sects and movements within the Judaism of his day and to the people, mainly Romans, even he called "heathens." At first glance, it hardly seems we can learn much from him on this subject.

Jesus also had no direct experience with many of the other vast questions we deal with today: runaway technology, genocidal weapons, AIDS, and the ethical issues involved in corporate takeovers, disinvestment, advertising, and insider trading. He never had to cope with the temptations that arise in filling out an expense account or an IRS form. But this misses the point. To be a disciple of Jesus does not mean to emulate or mimic him. It means to follow his "way," to live in our era the same way he lived in his—as a sign and servant of the reign of God. To "follow" Jesus does not require us to choose twelve disciples or to turn water into wine but to take his life project—making the coming of God's reign of Shalom real and immediate—our own. I believe that friendship among the peoples of the world faiths and the nurturing of a sense of "species consciousness" is an indispensable facet of the coming of God's Shalom. I also believe there are at least four ways in which the Jesus of the Gospels, he who "came preaching the Reign of God," provides useful guidelines for building such an interfaith consciousness.

The first is that a focus on Jesus moves the encounter from the theoretical level to the practical one. The reign of God is not an abstract ideal. It is a reality actualizing itself in history. Consequently, as soon as this Kingdom becomes the focus, we see that religions do not exist apart from their local manifestations. Further, these concrete expressions of a tradition vary markedly from place to place. Except in the minds of textbook writers, there is no such thing as Buddhism or Hinduism, or Christianity for that matter. There are only *persons* who think of themselves as Buddhists, Hindus, or Christians. Comparing classical religious texts can be misleading unless one understands what these texts mean to the actual people who chant them, study them, and try to live by them. And these meanings change from time to time and from place to place. Genuine interreligious dialogue occurs only when we recognize how a tradition actually shapes people's lives. Those who ignore this insight soon find themselves touring a never-never-land of "religions" that do not exist except in comparative religion monographs. To follow Jesus means to deal with specifics, not generalities.

Such a down-to-earth approach to interreligious conversation is anything but easy. It makes what was already an arduous undertaking even more difficult. Christians committed to dialogue with the people who live according to other faiths can no longer be content with the "library" versions of those traditions. Nor will it help to complain that the actual Buddhist or Islamic movements we meet today are not the real thing but decadent or "politicized" corruptions (as though "pure" editions existed once upon a time). The example of Jesus' own life demonstrates that any dialogue must take place with actual people. A so-called interreligious dialogue with the Platonic ideals of what this or that religious tradition ought to be in its pure essence leads nowhere.

The second way the Jesus of the Gospels facilitates interfaith dialogue is by reminding us that religion is always a mixed blessing. Jesus, after all, was fiercely opposed by many (not all) of the religious people of his day. His attacks on the misuse of religion remind us that, wherever religion exists, we can be sure that someone is trying to use the gods to dominate, frighten, or oppress someone else. Indeed, any honest attempt at interfaith dialogue must deal with the fact that our century has not only spawned hundreds of new religious movements but that some of those movements are destructive and some of the most demonic claim to be expressions of Christianity.

What are the limits of tolerance? Were the Christians of Japan being intolerant when they opposed the state Shinto that the military used during World War II to lead their nation to ruin? Was Bonhoeffer being narrow-minded when he refused to be cozily ecumenical with the *Deutsche Christen* who supported the Nazi effort to synthesize Christianity with the spirit of the German *Volk?* Should no one raise questions about human sacrifice, or consigning widows to their husbands' funeral pyre, or collecting Rolls Royces in the name of Christ? The more we think about it, the more obvious it becomes that a benign tolerance, which sees anything religious as good, will simply not do.

Intimidated by this need to "grade" religious practices, some gentle souls suggest that maybe we should simply declare a kind of moratorium both on proselytizing and on interreligious discussion. Why not just live and let live? The idea is not without its attractions.

But it is impossible. People travel today at the speed of sound, and ideas travel at the speed of light. It is idle to hope that various cultures and religions could simply leave each other alone. There will always be interraction. Some kind of encounter, even dialogue, is unavoidable. The hard question is how to enter into a genuinely open encounter without losing sight of the need to make judgments and, at times, even to take sides.

This is where the example of Jesus is most pertinent. Jesus was not a model of vacuous tolerance. He did make judgments about the faith of the people he met. In fact, he did so all the time. He argued with the pharisees and excoriated the rulers of the temple. But the key to Jesus' approach to any religious perspective was, "By their fruits shall ye know them." He seemed singularly uninterested in the doctrinal content or ritual correctness of the different religions he encountered. He was, however, terribly concerned about the practical outcome of people's spiritual commitments. He once told a pagan Roman he had not found such a faith as his anywhere in Israel.

Third, Jesus' example also reminds us that the search for human oneness-in-diversity in interreligious dialogue is not *only* a matter of making judgments. It also sometimes requires refraining from judgment. This has its rewarding and even its lighter side. When I was living among Tibetan Buddhists, for example, it took me some time to appreciate the frolicsome way they approach even the deepest tenets of their faith. They sometimes called it the "crazy wisdom." I found that, as a Christian, I eventually had to lay aside the notion that dialogue must always be serious. The same is true with the so-called primal religions. At a conference in Japan, a pioneer of Christian dialogue with tribal peoples once observed that Western Christians tend to be at ease only with those adherents of other faiths who are as precise and sober as they are. Perhaps we need to place the "theology of play" at the service of interfaith encounter, especially with Buddhists and those who used to be called "primitive" peoples. Jesus often responded to people's serious questions by rattling off a story, and some of his stories—like the one about the speck in the neighbor's eye and the two-by-four in my own—are downright hyperbolic. I am sure people laughed when he told them.

To insist that dialogue must always be about clear and distinct ideas is to impose a narrowly Western verbal-doctrinal style. What occurs, then, is nothing but a more subtle form of religious imperialism. Exchanging jokes and anecdotes is also a form of dialogue.

Can Christians allow themselves to enter into this friskier and more "ludic" expression of interfaith exchange? There's reason to believe that the tragic schism between the Byzantine and Latin churches deprived Western Christians of a tradition that preserved this roguish element. There was for many years in the Orthodox world the tradition of the holy fool. Harking back to Saint Paul's words in the Epistle to the Corinthians about being "fools for Christ," the holy fools were not only accepted but venerated. Alexander Syrkin describes, for example, one Symen, a contemporary of the Emperor Justinian I (527–65). Symen is said to have dragged a dead dog through the streets and then gone to the church and thrown nuts at the worshipers. Sometimes he would creep through the village on all fours, get himself beaten by a town ruffian, trip people as they walked, and stroll through the market with no clothes on. Apparently, the theological tactic behind all this tomfoolery was to awaken his surprised audiences from their lethargy, lampoon conventional values, and bring people to religious insight without accruing any praise or credit to himself.

When we look for an analogous tradition in Western Christianity, the closest we come is to Saint Francis and his earliest friars. Clearly, the behavior of the saint himself was viewed as mad by many of his contemporaries, beginning with his parents. Legend says that Francis, like Symen, stripped himself of the finery his well-to-do family had provided and stood naked in the town square, and that the citizens inveighed against him until the local bishop protected him. Francis said he wanted to "become naked" so he could "follow the naked Christ." But Francis also had a comic streak. As a boy, he had admired traveling troubadours. Later he called himself and his followers *joculatores Domini* (jesters of the Lord). Many of the stories about them handed down in *The Little Flowers* are strongly reminiscent of the capers attributed to the Russian holy fools. Once, for example, Francis is said to have sent Rufinus through the streets to the church to preach clad only in his underwear. On another occasion, the inimitable Brother Juniper cut the adornments and decorations from a church and gave them to poor people so they could get money to buy food. The famous pilgrimage Francis himself took through the battle lines of the crusading armies to visit the caliph was a classical fool's errand. The reason the Muslims did not kill him is that they also had a certain respect for holy madness.

In an interreligious dialogue, this crazy wisdom has an important theological meaning. It implies that the participants realize—as mystics also do—that even their best words fall far short of the divine reality, so far short as to be somewhat ridiculous. This insight undercuts distinctions that are very precious to the West: correct/incorrect, secular/sacred, wisdom/folly, purity/dirtiness. It thus points toward what mystical theology calls the *coincidentia oppositorum,* the ultimate union of what appear to be opposites.

The fourth way the Jesus of the Gospels helps facilitate interreligious encounter is that he teaches us to expect to find God already present in the "other," including the one with whom we are in dialogue, no matter how strange or unfamiliar that other's ideas or religious practices may seem. Christ meets us in and through the stranger. I have always known that this is true "in principle," but by participating in the dialogue I have learned it is also true in reality. To step into real dialogue, as Martin Buber knew, is to step onto holy ground. It invites both blessedness and pain. No one who enters—really enters—remains unaffected. If they do, there is room for doubt whether they have entered at all. Dialogue changes those who risk it. It upsets more than stereotypes and preconceptions about the "other"; it works an even more subtle transformation of the way I understand and live my own faith. To enter honestly into dialogue is to embark on a perilous personal voyage with no clear destination in view. Unforeseen things can happen. One of the risks is running the possibility of being viewed by one's coreligionists with suspicion or distrust. "Why do you want to bother with *them?*" Another is to find oneself asking questions, perhaps only inwardly, about what one's own faith really means, questions that would never have come up without the provocation of the other. The fearful gatekeepers who have insisted throughout the ages that "pure religion" can be maintained only in a ghetto or compound have not been entirely wrong. To expose one's tradition to dialogue is willy-nilly to open it to change, ferment, and internal debate. I believe God can and does speak to us through people of other faiths. And as people of faith have always known, when God speaks, mountains melt and the seas roar.

Christians have entered into serious dialogue with people of other faiths only very recently. As we have seen, one of the questions this conversation has sparked *within* Christianity itself concerns what Jesus means for the dialogue. But the question of what Christ means for our encounter with the other inevitably raises the even more basic one of what Christ means for us as Christians. It never fails. I invariably return from a conversation with a genuine believer in one of the other faiths with Christ's famous question to Peter ringing in my mind: "Who do you say that I am?" But, as I listen, I find I am not putting the question to the other. I am putting it to myself.

Perhaps the most unexpected thing I have learned in the dialogue with people of other religions is how important it is for me to keep in touch with those of my own faith community who remain suspicious and fearful of that dialogue. This has sometimes proven difficult, and I have often found it easier to converse with universally minded Buddhists or Hindus than with fellow Christians who not only dismiss such people as pagans but also want to dismiss me for not recognizing it. Still, I believe the critically important conversation among people of diverse faiths could founder and fail if we—the dialoguers—lose touch with our fellow believers who cluster on the particularistic side. We may not admit it, but we do need each other. They remind us that without the radical particularity of the original revelation, we would have no faith to share. We remind them that without the universal dream they falsify the message and diminish the scope of the original vision.

Multiple specters stalk the human enterprise today. We have reached a point where strife between nations and religions could lead to the final apocalypse. We need more than ever to doxologize the fragile oneness of the whole earth and all her inhabitants. Yet for men and women of faith, the sacred stories by which we hymn the unity of our species and its animal and cosmic neighbors need not be invented. Paradoxically, those stories and symbols are already embedded in the same traditions that sometimes threaten to tear us asunder. Our task is to claim these reminders of our common destiny from within the desperate sources that first gave them voice.

I invite my readers to journey with me through some of the discoveries and disappointments that have marked my attempts to cultivate the conversation with people of other faiths while trying to nurture the vital sources of the faith that motivates the conversation. From Jesus I have learned both that he is the Way and that in God's house there are many mansions. I do not believe these two sayings are contradictory. In fact I have come to see that only by understanding one can we come to understand the other.

2

The Gospel and the Koran

I will call her Fatima Hassan. That is not her real name. But since our meeting she has returned to a country where, I suspect, she would not want those in power to know much about her sojourn in America. Fatima's name appeared on my appointments schedule one morning several years ago after I had announced that I wanted to interview graduate students as possible teaching assistants in a course called "Jesus and the Moral Life." When she entered, dressed in the clean but casual Western clothes most overseas students at Harvard wear, I welcomed her and asked if she had had any previous teaching experience. She had indeed, she said, and handed me a neatly typed curriculum vitae replete with an imposing set of complimentary references about her ability as a teacher. In conversation she seemed relaxed and confident. Her own course record, studded with A's, and her replies to my questions suggested that she had a firm command of the material the course would cover. She also appeared enthusiastic about teaching it. I leaned back in my chair. I was about to say, "You're hired," when Fatima said, "There is one more thing I think you should know about me. I'm a Muslim."

I tried not to appear startled. Her real name, which was just as identifiably Muslim as the pseudonymn I have given her here, should have forewarned me. Somehow, I had just never expected that a Muslim would want to teach a discussion section in a course about Jesus. "Well . . . ," I said, in a slight delaying action, thinking that somehow I should ponder, at least for a few hours, a decision that seemed to carry with it such unforeseeable consequences—especially for the undergraduates who would end up in her weekly section meeting. But Fatima spoke before I could continue. "I realize it may seem odd to you," she said, with a smile, "but that's only because you Christians know so little about how much respect we Muslims have for Jesus." I told her she was right, at least in my case. At that time—though I have tried hard to rectify my ignorance since—I knew very little about Islam and even less about what Muslims thought about Jesus.

"The trouble is," Fatima went on, "that there is so little symmetry. We honor and even venerate Jesus, but Christians have a history of vilifying Muhammad." She did not seem angry, just eager to inform me about something I obviously did not know.

"Is that right?" I asked, beginning to feel just a little queasy about the direction the conversation was moving.

"Yes, it is," she said, "do you remember the awful description of Muhammad in Dante's *Inferno?*"

I told her I had read the *Inferno* in a sophomore humanities class twenty-five years before but could not honestly remember any reference to the Prophet.

"You should read it again," she said, still firmly, but with no sense of rancor, "and then try to imagine how a Muslim professor might feel if a Christian applied for a teaching assistant's position in a course on Muhammad. It's in canto 28."

That night at home I pulled down my copy of Dante's *Divine Comedy* and turned to the canto Fatima had mentioned. This is what I found:

> No cask without an end stave or a head
> E'er gaped so wide as one shade I beheld,
> Cloven from chin to where the wind is voiced.
> Between his legs his entrails hung in coils;
> The vitals were exposed to view, and too
> That sorry paunch which changes food to filth.
> While I stood all absorbed in watching him
> He looked at me and stretched his breast apart,
> Saying: "Behold, how I split myself!
> Behold, how mutilated is Mahomet!
> In front of me the weeping Ali goes,
> His face cleft through from forelock to chin;
> And all the others that you see about
> Fomenters were of discord and of schism;
> And that is why they are so gashed asunder."

As it turned out, I did engage Fatima as a teaching assistant, but to my great regret she was not able to accept the job. A few weeks after our conversation she was called home. "A family emergency," she explained to me on the phone. But she said it in a tone that suggested there were other factors at work as well.

I have never seen Fatima again, but since the memorable conversation in my office that day I have learned that odious Western images of Muhammad and of Islam have a long and embarrassingly honorable lineage. Dante places the Prophet in that circle of hell reserved for those stained by the sin he calls *seminator di scandalo e di scisma*. As a schismatic, Muhammad's fitting punishment is to be eternally chopped in half from his chin to his anus, spilling entrails and excrement at the door of Satan's stronghold. His loyal disciple Ali, whose sins of division were presumably on a lesser scale, is sliced only "from forelock to chin." There is scandal, too. A few lines later, Dante has Muhammad send a warning to a contemporary priest whose sect was said to advocate the community of goods and who was also suspected of having a mistress. The admonition cautions the errant padre that the same fate awaits him if he does not quickly mend his ways. Already in Dante's classic portrait, we find the image of the Muslim linked with revolting violence, distorted doctrine, a dangerous economic idea, and the tantalizing hint of illicit sensuality.

Nothing much has changed in the 600 years since. Even the current wave of interest in Eastern spirituality among many American Christians has not done much to improve the popular estimate of Islam. It is fashionable now in the West to find something of value in Buddhism or Hinduism, to peruse the Sutras or the Bhagavad Gita, to attend a lecture by a visiting swami or lama, even to try a little yoga or meditation. But Americans in general and Christians in particular seem unable to find much to admire in Islam. As G. H. Hansen observes, with only a modicum of hyperbole, in his book *Militant Islam,* the mental picture most Westerners hold of this faith of 750 million people is one of "strange bearded men with burning eyes, hieratic figures in robes and turbans, blood dripping from the amputated hands and from the striped backs of malefactors, and piles of stones barely concealing the battered bodies of adulterous couples." Lecherous, truculent, irrational, cruel, conniving, excitable, dreaming about lascivious heavens while hypocritically enforcing oppressive legal codes: the stereotype of the Muslim is only partially softened by Sufi wisdom stories or *The Arabian Nights.*

There is, of course, one important exception to the West's rejection of the religious value of Islam. This exception's most visible representatives are Elijah Muhammad, Muhammad Ali, and the late Malcolm X. Most Americans who seem genuinely drawn to the call of the minaret are black. But, given the racial myopia that continues to affect almost all American cultural perceptions, this exception has probably deepened the distrust most white Christians feel toward Islam. The dominant image was summed up brilliantly in a Boston newspaper's cartoon showing a Muslim seated in prayer. Over his head the balloon contained one word: "Hate!"

This captious caricaturing of Muslims and Arabs is not confined to the popular mentality. In his *Orientalism,* Edward Said describes a study published in 1975 of Arabs in American textbooks that demonstrates how prejudices continue to be spread through respectable sources. One textbook, for example, sums up Islam in the following manner: "The Moslem religion, called Islam, began in the seventh century. It was started by a wealthy businessman of Arabia, called Muhammad. He claimed that he was a prophet. He found followers among the other Arabs. He told them they were picked to rule the world."

This passage is, unfortunately, not atypical. Although phrased with some degree of restraint, it coheres all too well with the popular medieval picture of Muhammad as a sly trickster or the current comic-book depictions of the sated, power-mad Arab. Moreover, Dante's unflattering portrait of the Prophet was rooted in traditions that existed long before his time. These primal shadowgraphs have notoriously long half-lives, and they continue to darken our capacity to understand Islam to this day.

Allah works in mysterious ways. Through the stubborn geopolitics of oil, Westerners are being forced, like it or not, to learn more about Islam than they ever thought they would. Inevitably, this reappraisal has begun to include a rethinking of the relation between Islam and Christianity. In the fall of 1979, the World Council of Churches sponsored a conference on the subject in Kenya, and Christian scholars with direct experience of Islam were invited from all over the world. The results were mixed since, ironically, theologians from countries where Islam is a small minority seemed much more eager to enter into dialogue with their Muslim counterparts than did those from countries where Christians form a small minority in an Islamic world. But some kind of contact is inevitable, especially since the upsurge of immigration into Europe and the United States from Muslim countries. A couple of years ago, for example, the churches of a southern California community sponsored a dialogue evening where Christians and their Muslim neighbors could meet each other.

All such activities are welcome. But what about the shadowgraphs? Conferences and courses will help only if their participants become aware of the deep-seated, nearly archetypal images that subvert the whole enterprise from the outset. Along with study and analysis, a kind of cultural archaeology or even a collective psychoanalysis may be necessary if we are to leave Dante's *Inferno* behind and live in peace with our Muslim neighbors on the planet Earth. The question is, How can Westerners, and Christians in particular, begin to cut through the maze of distorting mirrors and prepare the ground for some genuine encounter with Muslims?

The first thing we probably need to recognize is that the principal source of the acrimony underlying the Christian-Muslim relationship is a historical equivalent of sibling rivalry. Christians somehow hate to admit that in many ways their faith stands closer to Islam than to any other world religion. Indeed, that may be the reason Muhammad was viewed for centuries in the West as a charlatan and an imposter. The truth is—theologically speaking, at least—both faiths are the offspring of an earlier revelation through the Law and the Prophets to the people of Israel. Both honor the Virgin Mary and Jesus of Nazareth. Both received an enormous early impetus from an apostle—Paul for Christianity and Muhammad for Islam—who translated a more particularistic faith into a universal one. The word "Allah" (used in the core formula of Islam: "There is no God but Allah and Muhammad is his prophet") is not an exclusively Muslim term at all. It is merely the Arabic word for God and is used by Arabic Christians when they refer to the God of Christian faith.

There is nothing terribly surprising about these similarities since Muhammad, whose preaching mission did not begin until he reached forty, was subjected to considerable influence from Christianity during his formative years and may have come close—according to some scholars—to becoming an Abyssinian Christian. As Arend van Leeuwen points out in his thoughtful treatment of Islam in *Christianity in World History,* "The truth is that when Islam was still in the initial stages of its development, there was nothing likely to prevent the new movement from being accepted as a peculiar version of Arabian Christianity." Maybe the traditional Christian uneasiness with Islam is that it seems just a little too similar. We sense the same aversion we might feel toward a twin brother who looks more like us than we want him to and whose habits remind us of some of the things we like least in ourselves.

The metaphor of a brother, or perhaps a cousin, is entirely germane. Muhammad considered himself to be in a direct line with the great biblical prophets and with Jesus. The title he preferred for himself was *al-nabi al-ummi,* "the prophet of the nations" (or of "the gentiles"). He believed he was living proof that the God who had called and used previous prophets such as Abraham and Job, neither of whom was Jewish, could do the same thing again. Later on, Muslim theologians liked to trace the genealogy of Muhammad back to Hagar, the bondwoman spouse of Abraham. The Old Testament story says that Hagar's giving birth to Ishmael stirred up such jealousy between her and Sarah, Abraham's first wife and the mother of Isaac, that Sarah persuaded Abraham to banish the bondwoman and her child into the desert. There Hagar gave up hope and left the child under a shrub to die. But God heard the child's weeping, created a well of water in the desert to save them both, and promised Hagar that from her son also, as from Isaac, he would "create a great nation." According to the symbolism of this old saga, the Jews and the Arabs (and by extension all Muslims) are the common offspring of Abraham (called "Ibrahim" in Arabic). This makes Christians and Muslims cousins, at least by legendary lineage.

The similarity between Christians and Muslims does not stop with religious genealogy. The actual elements of the Koran's message—faith, fasting, alms, prayer, and pilgrimage—all have Christian analogues. Despite its firm refusal to recognize any divine being except God (which is the basis for its rejection of Christ's divinity), Islam appears sometimes to be a pastiche of elements from disparate forms of Christianity molded into a potent unity. Take the Calvinist emphasis on faith in an omnipotent deity, the pietistic cultivation of daily personal prayer, the medieval teaching on charity, the folk-Catholic fascination with pilgrimage, and the monastic practice of fasting, and you have all the essential ingredients of Islam. All, that is, except the confluence of forces that, through the personality of Muhammad and the movement he set off, joined these elements in the white heat of history and fused them into a coherent faith that has attracted hundreds of millions of people.

Like Paul, who said his apostleship was to both Jews and gentiles, Muhammad believed his mission was twofold. He felt called by God to bring the law and the Gospel to the heretofore neglected peoples of Arabia. But he also felt he had a mission to those very peoples—Christians and Jews (whom he called "peoples of the book")—from whom the original message of salvation had come. In one important respect, therefore, Muhammad's mission was different from Saint Paul's. Since Muhammad carried on his preaching in the early decades of the seventh century, not only did he have to deal with a Judaism he considered corrupted (as Paul had too); he also had to face an even more corrupted form of Christianity. Fortunately for Saint Paul, since the Christian movement was only a decade or so old when he lived, he had to cope only with a few legalizers and gnostics. The infant church had not yet tasted the corruption that comes, perhaps inevitably, from power and longevity. From a certain Christian perspective, Muhammad was as much a reformer as an apostle. A prophet of the gentiles, he also saw himself as a purifier of the faith of all the "peoples of the book," Christians and Jews, calling them away from the ornate and decadent versions of the faith they had fallen into and back to its simple essence, at least as he understood it. There is always something of this urge to simplify, to return *ad fontes,* in any reformer. Muhammad was no exception.

No one should minimize the fact that in any genuine conversation between Christians and Muslims certain real differences in theology and practice will have to be faced—what scholars often call "rival truth claims." But such conflicting assertions can be properly understood only against the flesh-and-blood history that has somehow made them rivals. Religious teachings do not inhabit a realm apart. They mean what they do to people because of the coloration given to them by long historical experience. Therefore, a previous question has to be asked. If Christianity and Islam share such common roots and, despite real differences, some striking similarities, why have they grown so bitter toward each other over the centuries? Why did the average white American feel less sympathetic to Islam than to any other world religion even before our current flap with the ayatollahs?

The explanation for this hostility is not a pretty story. Its major lineaments can be indicated with the names of three figures who symbolize its most critical stages. The first is Alexander the Great, whose career corresponds to what might be called the prehistory of Christianity. The second is Constantine the Great, who exemplifies its early period. The third is Pope Urban II, who expresses its classical phase, one of the most formative in the Christian-Moslem interaction.

Christopher Dawson, the late Roman Catholic cultural historian, once remarked that "Muhammad is the Orient's answer to Alexander the Great." At first, this sounds like one of those wonderfully sweeping but highly improbable aphorisms. Muhammad, after all, lived and preached a full thousand years after Alexander. The prodigious Macedonian disciple of Aristotle conquered everything between Greece and northern India before he was thirty-three and spread the culture and values of Hellenism wherever his soldiers trod. But a thousand years is not a long time when one is dealing with cultural domination and the backlash it ultimately elicits. This is what Dawson had in mind.

Alexander did more than conquer everything before him. Unlike previous conquerors, who sought mainly booty and tribute, he wanted to convert his colonized peoples into Hellenists. Alexander's conquest mixed military, political, and religious power. It was obviously going to require a comparable fusion of elements to throw off his conquest. After a thousand years, that response finally came. It was Islam.

As Albert Memmi writes in his classic book *The Colonizer and the Colonized,* "The colonized can wait a long time to live. But, regardless of how soon or how violently the colonized rejects his situation, he will one day begin to overthrow his unlivable existence with the whole force of his oppressed personality. . . . He attempts to . . . reconquer all the dimensions which the colonization tore away from him." When the Islamic response to Roman-Hellenistic domination exploded in the early seventh century, the entire world was stunned by its vitality. In retrospect, however, we can understand its religious ideology in large measure as a mirror image of what it was overthrowing. Take its rejection of the divinity of Christ, for example. Alexander had allowed himself to be viewed as a divine being, a god-emperor, and this ideology persisted through centuries of European culture in one form or another. The Koran's strenuous insistence that there was only one God, and its rejection of all semidivine beings, must be seen at least in part as a rejection of the political use of Christology to sacralize various forms of human rule.

The Muslim rejection of the divinity of Christ is not just simpleminded monotheistic stubbornness. It began as "political theology." For the Arabians, living on what were then the outskirts of the Eastern Empire, it marked a rejection not only of the non-Semitic categories in which the doctrine of Christ's divinity were elaborated in the church councils (the "being of one substance with the Father") but also of the political hierarchy the doctrine helped to sanctify, especially in the Byzantine environment. When the Pantocrator Christ began to sacralize an empire in which the Arabians were the underdogs, their refusal of the doctrine made perfect sense. Alexander the Great had created the cultural imperium for which Christianity eventually supplied the sacred ideology. The Islamic revolt against this system was a revolt not against the Gospel as Muslims understood it but against what Christianity had come to be. Islam's implacable insistence on one God not only freed thousands of people from their fear of the evil jinn and united the feuding tribes of Arabia (and later a vast part of the known world) but also became a counter-ideology to the political function that Christian trinitarianism was beginning to serve. No "rival truth claim" debate between Christians and Muslims can begin until this history is recognized.

Islam began as a liberation theology, but, like Christianity, which had a comparable beginning, it could not resist the wiles of worldly power. As in the case of most successful liberation movements, Islam incorporated many of the cultural and political characteristics of its enemies. Though Muhammad was hounded out of Mecca by its local power elites, one hundred years after his death a glittering capital for the new Islamic empire was founded at Baghdad, the "Constantinople of Islam." Muslims became imperialists themselves, although in most instances they allowed Christians and Jews to practice their faiths. Forced conversions were rare. Above all, Muslims became the supreme masters and cultivators of the very Greek wisdom that had been imposed on them by Alexander. They became devout disciples of the same Aristotle whose zealous pupil had set out to spread his master's learning in their lands a millennium before. It was the Arabs, after all, who brought Aristotle back to the West and eventually to the cluttered desk of Thomas Aquinas. At its height, Islamic culture vastly outshone that of the Christian West, which most Muslims more or less accurately regarded as a barren outpost. But, at the same time, the original liberating impulse of Islam had begun to run out. Today, paradoxically, this very spoiling by success may provide a needed bridge between Christians and Muslims since Christians have experienced the same sad, familiar story in their own history.

Muhammad's judgment on the Christianity of his day is one of the great ironies of history. This Christianity, which began in the life of a Palestinian Jew who was executed because he was viewed as a threat to the Roman Empire and to the Hellenistically inclined rulers of his colonized nation, was seen a few centuries later by Muhammad, the prophet of another downtrodden nation, as the religious sanction for his own people's domination. What is remarkable about Muhammad is not that he rejected current theories about the divinity of Christ but that he did not reject Jesus himself. Rather, he tried, from his own vantage point, to bypass the caricature of the Gospel that imperial Christianity had elaborated and to reclaim the faith of a people much like his own who had once looked to Allah for justice and mercy.

Jesus, then, is another vital link between the two faiths. To this day, Jesus holds a central place in Islamic teaching and is sometimes even depicted as a kind of supreme exemplar of what is meant by "submission to God" (the meaning of the word "Islam"). In popular Islamic belief, Jesus often occupies an even more important position. Thus, many Muslims believe that when the long awaited "Twelfth Iman," whose name is al-Mahdi, finally appears to usher in the reign of justice on earth (not in the sky, incidentally), he will either be accompanied by Jesus or turn out to be the same one whose "coming in glory" the Christian creeds confess. Could the figure of Jesus become not an insurmountable barrier but a possible bridge between two kindred traditions that honor him in different ways? I think it could, but only if the ground can be cleared of spiteful stereotypes and the sibling rivalry can be held at bay.

Both Christianity and Islam began as visions of captive peoples who yearned for deliverance and caught a glimpse of hope in the promise of God. The two can understand each other only when both begin to acknowledge these common roots, step out of the long shadow of Alexander the Great, and try to learn from each other what has gone so terribly wrong over the years of their common history.

Constantine the Great, Roman emperor from 313 to 337 C.E., represents the historical turning point that eventually created the second great obstacle between Christians and Muslims. The Christian movement began not only as a message of hope to a colonized nation but also as the faith of the poor and the brokenhearted. Three centuries later, however, when the emperor Constantine beheld the cross shining across the sun and later claimed to have won the imperial throne with the help of Jesus Christ, all that changed. Although Saint Paul could write to one of his fledgling congregations that there were "not many wise, not many powerful" in their midst, and although the common name for Jesus' followers in those earliest days was simply "the poor," Constantine's well-timed and canny conversion totally altered all that for good. It is impossible to understand Muhammad's view of Christianity unless one remembers that he was basing it not on the Gospel accounts but on his observation of how the church was actually functioning in his world. By their fruits ye shall know them.

Muhammad claimed to be one of the poor, at least when he started, and he never tired of reminding his followers that he was only an illiterate camel driver. He saw his humble origins not as a disgrace but as wondrous proof that God could raise up from the very stones children unto Abraham. The *al-ummi* with whom Muhammad identified himself has a double sense. The word means not only "the gentiles," or "people without the Law," but also the unlettered, something close to the *am-ha-aretz,* the poor "people of the land" with whom Jesus sided against the learned scribes and the opulent rulers of the temple. The historian H. G. Reisman says that Muhammad was "a leader of the masses against the privileged minorities of wealth and sophistication." This may also explain in part the popular Islamic belief, baffling to many Christians, that every child is a "born Muslim." With growing up and education come sophistication and corruption. In the Koran, every person has an inborn, natural awareness of God, a notion similar to an idea Saint Paul defends in the first chapter of his Epistle to the Romans. We all start out pious but are misled by a fallen civilization and perfidious religions. It is the task of preaching to call us back to what we were, or were intended to be, in the first place.

The Koranic vision of a simple faith by which the poor and the unlettered can withstand manipulation at the hands of the powerful and the better educated makes Christians uncomfortable today, and understandably so. It is painfully reminiscent of the "Blessed are the poor" with which Jesus began the Sermon on the Mount and the subsequent "Woe to you rich" with which he made sure he was not misunderstood. The church has never completely lost its recognition of this aspect of its history. It surfaces repeatedly in such places as Simone Weil's life-shaking discovery that Christianity is essentially a faith of the poor or the Latin American bishops' declaration that the church's special responsibility is to stand with the jobless and landless. Nor has Islam, despite prodigiously rich oil sheikhs, ever completely lost this central core of its tradition either. Each faith will find it easier to appreciate the other when this special role of the *al-ummi* becomes the major rather than the minor theme of its message. In this respect, Christianity probably has more recovering to do than Islam has.

Pope Urban II, who occupied the throne of Peter from 1088 TO 1099, is the third great actor in the tragedy of Christianity's cumulative falling-out with Islam. He was an energetic reformer who became pope during a period of divisiveness in the church; his main challenge was to bring it into some semblance of unity. Like many other rulers before him, religious and secular, Urban hit on a surefire unifying idea. Realizing that nothing unites like an external foe, and inspired by requests from the beleaguered Christians of the East, he preached a holy war against the infidels who were then occupying the Holy Sepulcher and promised the fullest spiritual benefit to those who would take up the cross. Christians and other Americans who criticize the concept of the jihad, or holy war, and decry the taking of hostages and conversion at sword's point are right, of course. But it does not require much reading in this not-so-glorious chapter in Western Christian history to see that Muslims were neither the first nor the only guilty party in this department. In fact, there is at least one prominent school of historical scholarship that sees the first Muslim expansion not as a jihad but as a large-scale migration similar to the one that had brought the Germanic tribes into the Roman Empire from the other direction. The concept of holy war can be found in more than one Old Testament verse. It did not originate with Islam. To many Arabs it must have seemed the only sensible response to the not entirely pacifist manner in which the Christian empire dealt with its recalcitrant provinces and with those forms of Christianity, such as Nestorianism, that the bishops deemed unacceptable.

Like all wars, holy or unholy, the Crusades produced their quota of atrocities on both sides. They also produced countless incidents of generosity and unexpected interfaith respect. The mutual admiration that developed between Richard I of England and the theologically articulate Saladin, celebrated in legend, seems to have had a factual basis. Still, it was the Crusaders and not the Saracens who boasted that when they first took Jerusalem the blood of the infidels, including wives and children, flowed through the streets as deep as the horses' stirrups. Such memories do not die easily, and it is important to recall that, although Westerners would sometimes like to reduce the "wars of the cross" to tales of chivalry and late-night movie fare, for many Muslims the Crusades—Christian jihads—remain the most graphic expression of what the cross means. All the more amazing then, that even the Ayatollah Khomeini, talking to a group of visiting American clergy on Christmas Day, 1979, could ask why, as those who worship the wounded Jesus, Americans were so incapable of understanding a wounded people such as his own. Apparently, some feeling for the real meaning of the cross has survived in Islam despite the Crusades.

If it took Muhammad a thousand years to respond to Alexander the Great, perhaps it should come as no surprise that it has taken the Islamic peoples another 900 years to respond to Pope Urban II, Peter the Hermit, and the hordes of idealists, adventurers, and thugs who in successive waves burned and pillaged their way across Europe toward the Holy Land for nearly 400 years. True, some historians hold that the Crusades might never have occurred had it not been for the previous threat of militant Islam to the West. Still, once the Crusades began, they acquired a lethal momentum of their own. Christian armies started by burning the nearest ghetto and, when their attempts to seize the Holy Sepulcher did not fully succeed, turned their cross-bedecked banners toward the pagan Baltic peoples and the Albigenses of southern France. It is an ugly history. But until the sorry story of Crusade versus jihad is faced frankly and then replaced by a more generous and conciliatory attitude, the hatred and suspicion between Christians and their Muslim cousins can only escalate.

No discussion of the relations of Muslims and Christians can proceed very far without raising the parallel question of the equally long and similarly vexed interaction of Muslims and Jews. The Jewish historian S. D. Goitein is the leading scholar in the study of what he calls the "symbiosis" between Jews and Arabs. Goitein has spent a lifetime probing Muslim religious literature, the medieval Geniza (documents written in Hebrew characters but in the Arabic language), and the fascinating histories of the so-called Oriental Jewish communities—those of the Arab and Muslim worlds. His *From the Land of Sheba* is an anthology of Yemeni literature. It would be hard to find a more reliable guide to this intricate area.

Goitein believes that Islam is actually far closer to Judaism than to Christianity in its core ideas. In taking this position, he joins a debate that has been going on for years (the other side contending that the similarity with Christianity is more important). Goitein bases his case on the obvious fact that both Islam and Judaism are religions of the Holy Law and that Muslim law is in many respects similar to the Jewish Halakah, which he calls its "older sister." Both therefore differ, at least in this respect, from Christianity, which, with its emphasis on grace, has always harbored a certain suspicion of religious law (even though Christian theologians have managed to spin out yards of it over the years).

Goitein's "sister" image of the bond between Islam and Judaism should not be surprising when one bears in mind the saying, attributed to Muhammad, "You will follow the traditions of those who preceded you span by span and cubit by cubit—so closely that you will go after them even if they creep into the hole of a lizard." This colorful advice takes on even more significance in the light of the fact that there were large Jewish settlements in the city of al-Medina, the birthplace of the first Muslim community, and that the biographers of the Prophet almost all see in these communities, not an obstacle to the spread of Islam, but in fact wondrous evidence of Allah's merciful and providential preparation of the people for a monotheistic faith. As with Christianity, the early years of Islam seem in retrospect to have promised mostly fraternal—or in this case sororial—congeniality with Judaism. But again, the roiling history of Jewish and Islamic peoples has often turned familial ties into tribal vendettas. Must it always be so?

In his informative book *Jews and Arabs: Their Contacts through the Ages,* Goitein does what only a seasoned scholar ever dares to do. He compresses eons of history into one volume, risks a few well-grounded generalizations, and even hazards some guesses about the future. He divides the millennia-long give-and-take between these two people into four periods. The first, corresponding perhaps to the Alexandrian age of the Christian-Islam story, begins before historical memory and reaches up to the sixth century C.E. and the appearance of Islam. During this early period, a critically formative one for the Jews since it saw the compilation of both the Bible and the Talmud, Goitein believes Jews and Arabs had quite similar social patterns and religious practices. He firmly rejects any notion of a common Semitic race, however, as a modern idea concocted from the misapplication of a term invented by a German scholar in 1781 to denote a group of related languages, not "races" or even peoples. The distinction is an important one. There are several examples of peoples who for a variety of historical reasons now speak a language spoken by other peoples with whom they have no ethnic consanguinity at all. Black Americans are a case in point. Likewise, Jews and Muslim Arabs are related, according to Goitein, but by history and tradition, not by race.

The period from, roughly 500 C.E. to 1300 C.E. is Goitein's second one. He describes it as one of "creative symbiosis" in which early Islam developed in a largely Jewish environment. Although he agrees that Christian influences, coming especially from monastic groups, played some role in this primal period, he believes that Judaism was even more important, so much so that he is willing to say—with some reservations—that Islam appears to be "an Arab recast of Israel's religion." But the influence was not one way, and the impact of Islam and the Arabic language on Jewish thought and the Hebrew language was, he adds, at least as considerable. Goitein also reminds his readers that, although Jews experienced some legal disqualifications under Muslim rule, they almost always fared better than they did under Christian dominance.

Goitein's third period begins in about 1300, when the previously high-riding Arabs began to "fade out" of world history at the same time that the Oriental Jews began to fade out of Jewish history. During this phase, which lasted until about 1900, the Arab nations fell to various conquerors until the entire Arab world had become a colony of the modern West. Meanwhile, Jewish religious and intellectual life flourished in Europe, while Jews living in the beleaguered Muslim world, though they nurtured a rich internal culture, shared the suffering and obscurity of their Muslim neighbors.

The present period in Goitein's scheme begins in about 1900 with the coincidental revival of Jewish and Arab cultural and national identities, both influenced by the growing nationalism of nineteenth-century Europe. Since Zionism was an almost exclusively European (and American) movement, however, it was perceived by Arabs and other Muslims more as a new Western intrusion into the East, a pattern going back at least to the Crusades, than as something essentially Jewish, at least at the beginning. Shortly after the founding of the State of Israel, however, Israelis had to cope with an opposite and unexpected version of this "intrusion" as Jewish immigrants from Arab countries, the "forgotten Jews" of the previous period, streamed into Israel, making it less "European" with every passing day. The paradox of this apparent double intrusion was illustrated recently when an Oriental Jewish scholar living in Israel complained to a visitor about all the remarks he heard from his European colleagues lamenting the "Levantizing" of Israel. "How," he asked, "can you 'Levantize' something that is already the Levant?" His comment underscores Goitein's thoughtful prophecy that, since the future of Jewish-Muslim relations has everything to do with the relations between Israel and its Arab neighbors, Israel's internal policy toward its Oriental Jews and its Arab citizens will be of decisive importance. Whether or not this turns out to be true, remembering the roller-coaster history of Jewish-Muslim relations helps one not to become too depressed about the steep decline these relations have taken in recent decades. There have been downs before as well as ups, and it is not impossible that the tiny minority of Arab-Israeli citizens who are also Christians might eventually be able to play a conciliatory role. Likewise, though it seems farfetched today, the global Jewish community, with centuries of experience in the Christian and the Muslim worlds, might someday provide an essential link between these two faith traditions, both in some ways its offspring. In any case, whatever happens to facilitate the conversation that must go on among Christians, Jews, and Muslims is bound to benefit all three. Jews may help, but in the final analysis, given the role our religions play in both our cultures, no real rapport between the Arabs and the West seems possible unless Christians and Muslims make a more serious effort to understand each other.

Curiously, after being warned for years that our greatest enemies in the world were godless and atheistic, Americans are now faced with a challenge that emanates from profoundly religious sources. Although Islam has never accepted the dichotomy between religion and the civil polity that has arisen in the West, there can be little doubt that the present Islamic renaissance is not a deviation but an authentic expression of the elements that were there at its origin. So we are now told that, instead of atheists, we are dealing with "fanatics" or "Muslim fundamentalists." This language is not very helpful either. Can we rid ourselves of this destructive mode of discourse?

The small beginnings of Christian-Muslim dialogues at the local level that have begun to take place both in the United States and in Great Britain are signs of hope. When Presbyterians and Lutherans actually meet, share a meal, and converse with Muslim believers in their own communities, stereotypes inevitably begin to fade. But such closer contacts do not solve everything, and may dramatize some of the differences even more. One such cleavage that will inevitably emerge is the different position women occupy in the two faiths.

Fatima Hassan was not the first Muslim I ever met. I had already come to know several Afro-Americans who are a part of what they call the "Nation of Islam," what others sometimes refer to as "Black Muslims." But she was the first from the Islamic heartland. Only later did I come to appreciate that for me my first contact had been with a woman and, therefore, with one considered by many Westerners to be part of a victimized internal minority within a closed world of veils and harems. Such questions will inevitably arise. But how much do we in the West really know about the life of Muslim women?

Although I never saw Fatima again, I have met several other Muslim women, and the picture they paint, though surely not an attractive one for most Western women—or men—is considerably more complex than it first appears. Women are hardly equal under the law where Islam reigns, but already Muslim women are going back to the Koran to argue against the abuses they insist have been introduced since the time of the Prophet. They also frequently argue that for them liberation must take a different form than it does for their American and European sisters. Take for example *Hijab,* the Muslim custom of covering a woman's head, which is also referred to as *purdah*. For many years this practice was enforced by social custom, not by law, and in many countries Muslim women could choose when and where—and even whether—they chose to follow it. But in Turkey (1926) and Iran (1936) whatever choice they had was taken from them. Veiling was made illegal as a part of these countries' feverish attempts to mimic the values and customs of the West.

Then in 1979 Americans watched with amazement on television as millions of Iranian women returned to wearing the *chador*, often while carrying guns. Of course they wore them in part—but not entirely—because it was made unlawful not to. I say "not entirely" because there is considerable evidence that large numbers of young women in Iran saw the *chador* as a badge of revolutionary ardor, a visible symbol of their rejection of imperialism and the decadent values of the West. In the book *Women of Iran,* Farah Azari reports these remarks by an Iranian schoolgirl: "We want to stop men from treating us as sex objects, as they always have. We want them to ignore our appearance and to be attentive to our personalities and minds. We want them to talk to us seriously as equals and not just chase us around for our bodies and physical looks."

As improbable as it may seem to us in the West, many Muslim women feel that their customary dress code is actually liberating. It frees them from the anxious need to be sexually appealing. It equalizes distinctions between those with more or less money and between those who do and those who do not have a conventionally "pretty" physical appearance. It also identifies the wearer as a fighter against the decadent values she believes the West has tried to impose on her world. Thoughtful Muslim women often say that although they would like to be "freed from the veil," they do not want to become clotheshorses and marionettes to the changing whims of Western fashion. Nor have they been persuaded that earning three-quarters of what men do or the "consecutive monogamy"—spiced with extramarital liaisons—that has become the practice here in the West is necessarily that great an improvement on their current marital status.

Still, in all these questions, the voices of the great majority of Muslim women are still to be heard from. They will come. And when they do, they might very well activate the now largely stalemated conversation among Christians, Jews, and Muslims that is so moribund today, in part because men have done all the talking and, on all three sides, women are hardly a part of it.

Sometime soon a real conversation must begin. Perhaps the moment has come to set aside Dante, Urban II, and the rest; to remember instead the two children of Father Abraham, from both of whom God promised to make great nations; to recall that Jesus also cast his lot with the wounded and wronged of his time; to stop caricaturing the faith of Arabia's apostle; and to try to help Christians, Jews, and Muslims recover what is common to them in a world that is just too small for any more wars, especially holy ones.

3

Christ and Krishna

What we in the West call "Hinduism" is in reality a vast congeries of rituals, folk customs, contradictory metaphysical theories, and ascetic practices that have in common mainly the fact that they all subsist side by side on the Indian subcontinent. The word "Hindu" itself is a medieval Persian one derived from the Sanskrit *Saindhava,* which means a person who dwells on the Sindhu or Indus River. Someone once called India the "land of a million gods." But if there is one divinity who excels all the others in preeminence and popularity, one who in his widespread appeal corresponds to Christ among Christians, it is surely the sky-blue Lord Krishna, the bejeweled flute player and paramour of the goat girls who is believed by millions of Hindus to be an embodiment of the supreme god Vishnu.

One day several years ago, I found myself a lot closer to Krishna than I had ever expected to be. It happened when I accepted an invitation from a group of American devotees of Krishna to join them in New York for one of their principal holidays, the Festival of Chariots. I said yes, in part because

I have found that participating in the celebrations of other religions often provides a better way to savor their inner meaning than does exchanging ideas around a polished conference table. Still, I could hardly have foreseen all I was in for. I arrived in New York the day before the festival. The next morning, to my total surprise (although with my full agreement), I found myself riding down Fifth Avenue on a fifty-foot-high wooden cart topped with a shimmering red silk canopy and a glistening gold dome. Furthermore, I was seated alongside a replica of the Hindu divinity Jagannatha (which means "Lord of the Universe"), who is believed by many Hindus to be none other than Krishna himself in his form as Daru-brahman ("God manifested through wood"). I knew I would enjoy the festival but I hardly expected to share the royal chariot with the sky-blue Lord himself.

I was not the only human being riding on the celestial cart. Seated around Jagannatha-cum-Krishna on the same vehicle were two other bemused American scholars of religion dressed in proper ties and jackets who—like me—had been invited as special guests. Swaying next to them sat a handful of saffron-robed leaders of the growing American Hindu community. It was a gorgeous summer day, and our cart was tugged past the Plaza Hotel and Bergdorf Goodman's by hundreds of willing haulers, including multitudes of beaming members of New York's growing Indian ethnic community in gleaming white dhotis and colored kurtas, dozens of American devotees of Krishna, and a number of random bystanders who apparently thought it looked like fun. After ours came two more slightly less spectacular carriages. The second bore Subhadra, Krishna's sister, and a third his brother Balarama. As we all rode sublimely along, clouds of incense sweetened the fumy air of Gotham, and specially designated devotees cooled the deities with horsetail fans or pushed back low hanging traffic lights with long wooden forked poles. Thousands of people witnessed the parade, and, at its climax beneath the Washington Arch in Greenwich Village, devotees served a free vegetarian feast to over a thousand guests, bystanders, and curiosity seekers.

Some Indians hope that the Festival of Chariots will eventually take its place—along with Saint Patrick's Day for the Irish, the Cinco de Mayo for Mexicans, and Columbus Day for Italians—as one of the numerous festive times that remind us of the religious and cultural diversity of America. On the day we rode through Manhattan, carts also rolled along Regent Street through London to Trafalgar Square, up the grades of San Francisco to Golden Gate Park, and through the boulevards, vias, and avenues of other cities throughout the world. It used to be possible to think of "Hinduism" as an exclusively Indian religious tradition. But now, Jesus has his devotees in Calcutta and Bombay, and Krishna and Siva have theirs in Sydney and in Lima (and even—as recent news stories report—in Moscow). Hinduism is no longer something foreign or exotic, and dialogue between Christians and Hindus can no longer be viewed as optional.

The Festival of Chariots was introduced into the Western world in 1967 by the followers of A. C. Bhaktivedanta Swami Prabhupada in order, as they put it, "to establish ancient India's Krishna conscious culture around the world *on its own terms*—not watered down, but as it is." Like the Indian religious tradition itself, however, the festival is very old. Legend claims it goes back thousands of years to a visit Krishna himself made to Kuruksetra in the Orissa section of eastern India during a lunar eclipse. According to the old account, Indradyumna, the king who ruled Kuruksetrạ, was so inspired by the divine visit that he commissioned a sculptor to carve Krishna's likeness as well as those of Balarama and

Subhadra, so he could convey them through the streets like royalty. As the artist slowly labored in a locked room, the king became increasingly impatient to see the results. Finally, he broke the door down, only to find the three wooden figures unfinished. The intrusion bothered the sculptor so much that he refused to go on with his task, so the three deities were carted around the city in their incomplete forms, just as they are today.

The deities do appear unfinished. Indeed, to some people this rough-hewn appearance makes them appear comic or surrealist. One New York observer who witnessed the chariots arriving in Greenwich Village told me he thought Jagannatha, with his black skin, huge circular eyes, face-wide grin, and flower garlands, looked "like Mickey Mouse in drag." I don't think the Indian devotees would have been annoyed by the remark—at least not on this day. For Ratha-yatra (the Indian term for Festival of Chariots) is a time for welcoming, blessing, and feeding everyone, including skeptics. As canto 1, chapter 11, of the Srimad-Bhagavatam, the scripture of this branch of Hinduism, puts it: "To receive the Lord Krishna there were all grades of population, beginning from Vasudeva, Ugrasena and Gargamuni . . . down to the prostitutes and *candalas,* who are accustomed to eat dogs. . . . As pure living entities, all are the separated parts and parcels of the Lord, and thus no one is alien. . . . The Lord is equally affectionate to all His parts and parcels, despite material gradation. . . . No one is rejected by the Lord from the Kingdom of God."

I saw no one eating dogs, but I admit the crowd in Manhattan on that particular day was lushly heterogeneous. No one objected when the devotees showered flower petals, greetings, blessings, and food on anyone who came within range. Some Hindus believe that even to cast one's eyes on the Ratha-yatra carts brings with it an enormous infusion of good karma, maybe even enough to escape the wheel of birth on this very turn. If this be true, it is worth pondering the fact that, because of this Festival of Chariots, several thousand taxi drivers, tourists, policemen, shoppers, and probably even a few prostitutes may not have to contend with the vicissitudes of even one more incarnation on planet Earth.

I was a guest at Ratha-yatra because, as a Christian student of Asian religions in America I welcome the new meeting of faiths that the Western migration of orientally inspired movements is making possible today. Not only have Americans been "turning East," but Eastern religions have been coming West. Since I wanted to learn as much as I could during the Festival of Chariots I resided at the Hare Krishna Temple in New York. Each day of my stay I arose for the liturgy that begins at 6:00 A.M. with the garlanding, feeding, and bathing of the Temple deities. As the devotees prayed and chanted, then sat on the floor and listened to an exposition of the Hindu Scriptures while the Manhattan traffic swirled by outside, I became aware that today we have the opportunity for a "larger ecumenism" than previous generation has had. The fact that hundreds of New York residents from Delhi, Calcutta, and Bombay came out to join the American devotees in pulling the chariots says something: Krishna is now at home in America. Hindus—both those of Indian descent and more recent converts—now live not across the ocean but down the street. And they are not invisible. A fifty-foot cart emblazoned with a billowing canopy is not exactly subtle. Whatever else one may say about Hare Krishna devotees—and much has been said—they tend to be very visible.

My interest and curiosity about Vaishnava Hinduism had begun two years before the Festival of Chariots when three devotees appeared in my Cambridge, Massachusetts neighborhood, knocking on doors and selling devotional books. Unlike most of my neighbors, I did not say, "Thank you, no," but invited them in for a conversation. They accepted, and that day I knew the religious map of the world was changing. Like most people in the United States, I knew very little about religious traditions from the East. This may seem astonishing when you consider the fact that I have a Ph.D. in religion. But the explanation is simple. I finished my formal academic work before many Americans "turned East" or Oriental faiths came West, at a time when Asian religious texts were not a required part of advanced theological studies. My training, up to that point, had been almost entirely in Western religions. So the visit by the devotees to my home became what theologians call a "paradigmatic event."

This term is an important one in Christian theology. It means an ordinary occurrence that comes to have more than ordinary significance, one that somehow reveals more than others do of God's purpose in the world. Devotees of a religious tradition stemming from north India knocking on my door in Cambridge became for me a sign that something important was happening. For centuries, Christian missionaries have journeyed to the Orient to teach people about Christ. But here was an instance of the East coming West. In the careers of Swami Prabhupada, who introduced Krishna devotion to the United States, or of Swami Muktananda, who brought another tradition of Indian spirituality, one sees a Hindu version of the stories of such Christian missionaries as David Livingstone and Mateo Ricci who went halfway around the world to bring Christianity to cultures where it had not been known before. And in the lamentable tale of Rajneesh and his ill-fated settlement in Oregon, one can see that the terrible reputations some Christian missionaries earn for themselves in heathen lands can easily be matched by Asian charlatans who land here. The consequence of all this is that the old "sphere of influence" solution for religious pluralism, which gave the West to Christianity, the Middle East to Islam, India to the Hindus, and so on, won't work anymore.

Still, it was in India itself that I really came to know Krishna. After that first encounter in Cambridge and the New York Festival of Chariots, I visited several Krishna temples in California, Boston, and Florida. I lived for short periods in some of them and participated—insofar as I could—in their devotions. I read much of the social, scientific, and historical commentary on Vaishnava Hinduism and studied the Bhagavad-Gita and the Srimad-Bhagavatam. So I was somewhat familiar with what Christians would call the "canonical sources" of devotion to Krishna. But hardly any of this prepared me for my visit to Vrndavana, the pilgrimage city in India that is sacred to all Krishna devotees. Previously, I had only heard about and read about the sky-blue flute player. In Vrndavana I actually met him.

My journey to India was the result of a chain of events that began in 1977 when there appeared in one of my advanced classes at Harvard a man named Shrivatsa Goswami, the son of a Vaishnava priest of the Radha-ramana Temple of Vrndavana. I first came to know Goswami as a sophisticated and credible interpreter of Hinduism and especially of his own Caitanya Vaishnava tradition. As we slowly became friends, I also learned that he was a direct descendant of a disciple of one of the original disciples of the great Hindu saint and teacher Lord Caitanya. A remarkable reformer, who lived at about the same time as Martin Luther, Caitanya is considered to be the founder of the modern Krishna movement in India. Shrivatsa himself also lived in Vrndavana, where his family still maintains the temple; and, as I learned about his life, I found myself wishing that someday I could see his temple and home. A few years later I did, and that visit gave me an exposure to the inside of the Vaishnava tradition most people in America never get. From this inner angle I came to see that, although Krishna seems to be at home in Manhattan, he is infinitely more at home in Vrndavana.

Vrndavana is a small city easily reached by a short train ride from New Delhi. I arrived on a cool October day and discovered almost instantly that it is impossible not to sense the presence of Krishna there. The city is crammed with temples, some no more than store fronts, others occupying several blocks. Some sort of devotional exercise seems to be going on somewhere every minute. Drums and finger symbols thump and jingle. Pilgrims arrive in battalions. Brightly robed priests and ragged holy men jam the dirt streets. Cows wander freely. The acrid sweet smell of hundreds of dung fires hangs everywhere, and the spirits of Krishna and his consort, Radha, seem to hover like a heavy jasmine perfume on the thick air.

The different temples in Vrndavana display their own distinctive imagery of the various facets of Krishna's love for Radha and hers for him. Even the seemingly transient elements of the passion that bound these two classic lovers together—jealousy and loneliness and anger—are faithfully depicted and celebrated. One whole temple is devoted to "Radha's pique," the petulance she is said to have felt about something Krishna did. It is impossible to stroll through the temples of Vrndavana without beginning to appreciate in a new way the infinite forms the love of God takes and the myriad vehicles through which it touches people.

Vrndavana also expanded my appreciation for the omnipresence of God in the world. Hindus believe that God is in all things, that even in the evanescent moods of youthful lovers something of the divine shines through. God irradiates all situations and all activities. In semirural Vrndavana—if not in noisy New Delhi—the traditional Indian link between immanence and transcendence seems unbroken. How long this antique unity will survive, however, is a serious question, and pondering it made me wonder whether such a fragile fabric will survive the galloping industrialization that is transforming all India. In Vrndavana I sometimes wondered—sadly—if I were witnessing a type of classical Hinduism future generations will only read about in books. I sometimes caught myself musing—with a kind of anticipatory nostalgia—about the lost paradise this town would someday be.

But Vrndavana has its shadowy side too. One day I took a walk by myself along some streets I had not explored before. Turning a corner by a decaying temple, I found myself in a narrow alley bordered by what appeared to be the outer wall of an old building on my left. It stood about forty feet high and was marked along its roadside surface with a series of twenty or thirty narrow cavelike indentations, about six feet high, ten feet across, and no more than fifteen feet deep into the wall. In each recess I saw the figure of a woman, dressed in what seemed to be patches of rags. The women were crouched over tiny stoves, huddled in the corner of the cave, or lying on tattered pieces of bed padding. At first I stopped and gaped at the surrealist montage of flickering flames and grotesque forms. But soon the utter wretchedness of the stone hovels and their occupants made me walk more briskly and pass by as quickly as I could, averting my eyes. I did not want to be a voyeur.

Somehow I sensed that I had come on a quarter of their city the Goswami family would rather I had not seen, so I did not mention it that night at our splendidly prepared and elegantly served dinner. The next day, however, I ran across an American friend, an anthropologist who was passing through Vrndavana on his way to another village. I discreetly asked him about the women in the crevices. He smiled grimly and told me it was probably just as well that I had not raised the question with my hosts. The women, he explained, were widows who had come to Vrndavana after their husbands died to live out their remaining years. In fact, he told me, they made up nearly a quarter of the town's population. Their harsh way of living, he said, was something Hindus had a hard time explaining to foreign visitors.

A Hindu wife, it seems, is the embodiment of a quality highly prized by Indians that we usually translate into English by the word "auspiciousness" (*magala* in Sanskrit). The mark Indian women wear on the center of their foreheads at least initially signified this *magala,* though for many today it has lost its original meaning. But the catch is this: the continuing auspiciousness of a Hindu woman depends on her ability to keep her husband alive. If he dies before she does, which is not at all unusual in a society where husbands are often much older than their wives, the woman loses her auspiciousness. She must then erase the mark from her brow. Indeed, according to classical texts, the only way she could retain her *magala* was to join her husband on the funeral pyre in what the Indians call *suttee.* This custom was outlawed many years ago by the British and continues to be illegal. It is discouraged by most Hindus today, but sometimes it still occurs in remote sections of India. A woman who participates in *suttee,* according to the old custom, will not lose her *magala* because she is never a widow. The instant of the soul's flight from the body in the flames is the critical one, and at that sacred moment the pair would be together.

The idea of auspiciousness is one of the hardest for non-Hindus to grasp. Sometimes *magala* seems to mean little more than what we would call good luck. But as Frederique Marglin has shown in *Wives of the God-King,* her pioneering study of the *devadasis,* or temple dancers, of Puri, it means something much more than that, and its centrality in the Hindu universe helps make sense of many things that previous schemes of interpretation could not. Formerly, most Western scholars, relying mainly on written texts and on male informants, interpreted Hindu culture on the basis of a status scale running from purity (the Brahmins) to impurity (the outcasts or untouchables). But this model failed at certain critical points. It could not explain, for example, why the temple dancers Marglin studied were viewed at one and the same time as both impure (because they were believed to engage in ritual sexual intercourse) and auspicious (they were invited to perform at weddings and other ritual occasions where good luck is important). Marglin, in conversations with the *devadasis* of Puri, discovered that auspiciousness is quite a different quality from purity. It has to do, not with moral rectitude, but with health and well-being and with "all that creates, promotes and maintains life." In fact, as it turns out, purity and status are not approprite categories at all in the lives of Hindu women. They are viewed as male values.

Marglin's work explains something that had puzzled Western students of Hinduism for a long time, namely, why certain activities that are regarded as impure—such as birth or menstruation—are also felt to be auspicious. The *devadasis* Marglin studied rank quite low in caste, and the fact that they are perceived to engage in a high level of sexual activity means that they bear the stigma of impurity. But at the same time they are believed to be incarnations of the goddess Lakshmi and are actually worshiped as such by pilgrims in Puri. Furthermore, they never lose their auspiciousness because they are all the wives of the god Jagannatha, the same embodiment of Krishna with whom I had once ridden from Central Park to Washington Square; and, since a god never dies, they never become widows. Marglin shows that the quality of *magala* is enormously elusive. It does not attach itself permanently to any particular object or action. What is auspicious may suddenly be transformed into what is inauspicious and vice versa. Indeed, it is this very mercurial and chameleon-like quality that renders *magala* so powerful.

In that dank back street in Vrndavana I had obviously run across a massive clump of auspiciousness-become-inauspiciousness, a colony of widows who had come to the holy city to live out their last years. But were they living them out in misery? Was it an awful injustice spawned by a horrible religious system that had consigned them to these fetid caves? Once again, it seemed to me, the patriarchal control of the myths and practices of a religion—this time Hinduism—has succeeded in making life miserable for women. I had to bite my tongue when I returned to my host's home after meeting my anthropologist friend. I kept wanting to make some caustic remark about what I had seen or to ask where was the much-touted mercy and compassion of Krishna if he countenanced this doleful practice.

But I said nothing. I knew that these widows, as miserable as they looked to me, were living at roughly the same level as a male *sunyas,* an ascetic who has voluntarily chosen to subsist on the simplest of food and provisions. *Sunyasis,* though they would hardly be invited to weddings as good luck charms (indeed their presence on such an occasion would be an omen of misfortune), are nonetheless regarded as the pinnacle of holiness by devout Hindus, perhaps because a *sunyas* has done something that ordinary people believe is spiritually important for everyone—renounce the comforts of the world—but that these same ordinary people do not feel ready for, at least not in this incarnation. Further, to challenge my hosts about the widows in Vrndavana might have invited a discussion about what value Christianity has attached to women, a conversation that could have gone on to the Inquisition's treatment of witches and a host of other grisly topics. I decided I was not ready for that quite yet, at least not in Vrndavana.

Nevertheless, the gasp I let out when I turned into the street of lost *magala* still returns to my throat at times. With it comes a train of thoughts leading me to recognize that so much of what we now call interreligious dialogue remains a truncated conversation among men about the male versions of the great religious traditions of the world. Only recently have women's voices—from the harem, from the back of the synagogue, from the lesser offices to which they have been consigned in the Christian churches, and from the street of the widows—begun to make themselves heard. As they do, everyone begins to discover an Atlantis of faith that male scholars have scarcely noticed. Exploring that submerged continent will make a huge difference in the dialogue. In her study of the temple dancers, Marglin learned that *sakti,* which is usually translated blandly as, perhaps, "female power," is not only nonhierarchical in Hinduism but actually antihierarchical. It is not control of others—as power is conceived of in nearly all political systems, East and West—but the capacity to bring forth life. As such, it has its equivalents in all cultures. Released, it could shatter and renew the existing patriarchal structure of male-dominated religions and societies. It could also turn the cautious dialogue between Christians and Hindus inside out.

I never exchanged a word with the widows of Vrndavana. I spoke almost entirely with men, who—as they do in most religious traditions—did not hesitate to speak both for themselves and for women. But I am convinced that, when women become full partners, the interreligious dialogue will change, so much so that what is now going on will be regarded as only an insufficient and misleading beginning.

I eventually left Vrndavana, leaving both the timeless temples and the sorry street of the widows behind. But I was determined not to forget my visit there and equally determined to learn more about Caitanya Vaishnavism, the branch of Hinduism I had met there. But when I got home I discovered that finding out about that tradition was not so easy. Most of its texts still remain untranslated, and books about it in English were not easy to come by. The reason is that for many years Vaishnavism, despite the fact that it is one of the largest Hindu "denominations," has been virtually ignored in American teaching about Indian religion. Instead, the school that has dominated the teaching about Hinduism here is a more philosophical one called Advaita Vedanta. This latter tradition established itself in our country early in the nineteenth century when it attracted the attention of Ralph Waldo Emerson and the transcendentalists, and it was later espoused by Annie Besant, Swami Vivekananda, and the founders of the Vedanta Society. Unfortunately, the massive influence of these formidable interpreters resulted in the downplaying of Vaishnavism and thereby produced a highly distorted view of the full complexity of Indian religious traditions—as if Indians were to know Christianity only through one small and very sophisticated strand of its life.

Vaishnavism also faces another problem in America: its structural similarity to pietistic Christianity make it both intriguing and forbidding. The similarity may even explain my own fascination with it. Both traditions, for example, cherish the idea of a personal God who becomes incarnate in a particular figure, reveals who God is, and elicits a form of participation in the life of God. At first the similarity between this pattern and the role of Christ in Christianity seems, once more, to make Jesus a bridge rather than a barrier. But there is another side: precisely because of its structural kinship to Christianity, Vaishnava Hinduism can be more, not less, threatening to Christians. This is not unusual. In fact, in many cases the discovery of a religious tradition that is strangely similar to one's own can elicit suspicion. Something can be too close for comfort.

People become interested in other religious traditions for a variety of reasons. For example, I tend to respond to movements with a strong emotional component. This is why I was attracted to Vaishnavism, with its vivid imagery and quasi-erotic symbolism. On the other hand, I think I know why Vedanta, the other variety of Hinduism, appealed to Emerson: it is basically cerebral, and, despite the Concord poet's lifelong celebration of "feeling," he always remained an intellectualizer. Vedanta is a Hinduism for thinkers. One can ponder and puzzle over it endlessly, but the emotional edge is not as biting or exuberant as that of Vaishnavism. One does not dance or clang finger cymbals at a meeting of the Vedanta Society.

But a Christian who was reared—as I was—in a pietistic tradition can sometimes feel strangely at home with Krishna devotion. Like pietistic Christianity, it celebrates the devotion of the heart. Being reared in a more sentient form of Christianity enables one to be more receptive to Vaishnava spirituality than would be the case, for example, if one were nurtured in a liberal Protestantism with a strong emphasis on the rationality and reasonableness of faith and a suspicion of emotionality.

Studying Vaishnavism and Vedanta makes it evident that, in comparing Christian with Hindu theology, one has to be careful to specify which "Christianity" and which "Hinduism" are being considered. It suggests that we must get away from the idea that, in the ideal interreligious dialogue, we will have all the Hindus on one side of the table, all the Christians on another side, all the Jews on a third, and all the Muslims at a fourth. The truth is that there are elements within any of these movements that are more like those within another tradition than they are like certain elements within their own. There are many examples of such crisscrossing. For example, those forms of Christianity that support the transformation of earthly existence are more like Shin Buddhism than they are like other forms of Christianity that completely transcendentalize the action of God into a future life or a different world. Shin Buddhism in turn is more like some branches of Christianity, at least in this respect, than it is like Zen Buddhism.

This is the paradox: some Christians or Hindus or Buddhists feel closer to certain adherents of another tradition than they do to some members of their own. And this discovery shakes up the positioning of the chairs around the "dialogue" table. It has even led some scholars to suggest that it is misleading even to speak about "Hinduism" or "Christianity" or "Buddhism" as such. We should refer, they say, only to various theological or psychological types within the different faiths. We should talk about the pantheist, the monotheist, the monist, the pietist, and the fundamentalist "strands" within each of the traditions. Thus, it is said, a mystically inclined Hindu or Buddhist might feel much closer to a mystical Christian than to another Hindu or Buddhist, and vice versa. This may have been what Thomas Merton was touching on in the last years of his life when he found himself preferring the monks of other traditions to the non-monks of his own. Conversely, I met a Thai Buddhist in Japan who told me he feels much closer to socially committed Christians than he does to the world-denying ascetics of his own faith.

This repositioning of the chairs in interreligious dialogue is also recommended by those who engage in the "structuralist" analysis of religion. These scholars tend to deemphasize the doctrinal content of any particular religious phenomenon and look instead at the formal aspects—symbol, sacrifice, or ritual—and their analogues in other traditions. I am sympathetic with this approach to comparative religion, but only up to a point. My reservation is that, despite my proclivity to the emotional side of faith, I recognize that people are characterized not only by the feelings they enact in rituals but also by what they believe to be true about the world. The fact that Krishna devotees relate to Krishna as disciples in a way that is similar to the way Christians follow Jesus Christ, for example, can lead one to overlook the fact that there are real differences between what Krishna means to his disciples and what Christ means to his. In dialogue one learns eventually that we must talk about differences, not in any derogatory way but in order to recognize that the content of the teaching—what the disciple learns from the Lord—is not simply secondary.

Let me give an example of how a structuralist analysis can both illuminate and mislead. Several years ago, when I was teaching in West Virginia, my students and I visited the famous Krishna temple in Moundsville and immediately noticed several surprising similarities between what one might call "Appalachian folk religions," such as pentecostalism, and Krishna consciousness. Both faiths attach considerable importance to emotional devotion to God, to praising the Lord's name through singing and playing instruments. Both emphasize puritanical virtues and practice certain forms of self-denial, such as no drinking, smoking, nonmarital sex, or gambling. Neither puts much emphasis on the transformation of the present world into a religiously ideal world, such as the Kingdom of God, and both traditions have what a liberal religionist would consider a somewhat uncritical attitude toward Scripture and are reluctant to use historical-critical approaches to understand religious texts. But does this mean that Lord Krishna, the bejewelled gay-blade god of North India, could find a home among West Virginian tongue speakers? No, not so easily. Though the two traditions appear to be structurally analogous in many respects, the conversations we had with Krishna devotees and with Appalachian pentecostalists soon convinced us that the inner meaning of their outwardly similar practices is actually quite different. These observations taught us that structural analyses, though often helpful, should be used with caution. They may lead us to think we spot similarities where they do not in fact exist and to lose sight of the differences between what a religion claims is true.

Still, this does not mean Hindus have nothing to teach Christians. Indeed, after my return from India, I began to ask myself whether there were any parts of Vaishnava Hinduism that might nourish Christianity. Here, my thoughts began to move in an unexpected direction. My discovery of the mysterious power of *sakti,* especially as it is pictured in the relationship between Krishna and Radha his consort, forcibly raised the question of the appropriate place of the erotic in human life. This is an area that not only remains undeveloped in most of Christianity but has often been repressed and forbidden. My encounter with Krishna and Radha made me ask why?

Some scholars believe the Gospels we now have in the biblical canon were placed there at the expense of the recently discovered "gnostic Gospels," in which the feminine quality of God and the relationship of Jesus to Mary Magdalene and other women were more fully pictured. As Elaine Pagels has shown in her splendid book *The Gnostic Gospels,* the excision left us with a bowdlerized New Testament. Although there is more than a hint of this uxorious genre in the Hebrew Scriptures (in the Song of Solomon, for example) it seems to have become a forbidden theme in the period of the formation of the New Testament. It never died out completely, of course, and we find some rather explicit sexual imagery among medieval Christian women mystics and in some familiar hymns and devotional writings. Hadewijch of Flanders includes this sentence in her description of how Christ comes near in prayer: "He came himself to me, took me entirely in his arms, and pressed me to him." There is also John Wesley's famous hymn "Jesus Lover of My Soul," which includes the line "Let me to thy bosom fly." But in the Christian devotion the erotic is more often disguised and sublimated. The result is that the whole area of sexuality as a realm in which the divine is present, and from which we draw metaphors for our relationship with God, has been almost totally excluded from more formal Christian theological reflection. Christians usually identify God's love as *agapē;* Vaishnava Hindus may have something to teach us about the presence of God in *eros.* They see the love between Radha and Krishna as the central paradigm of God's love for human beings and of their love for God. They see *agapē* and *eros* not as opposites, but as parts of a continuum.

Vaishnavism may also be able to contribute to another impoverished area in our biblical sources: the feminine quality of God. Recent biblical scholarship has shown that our standard translations have misled us badly about the gender of references to the Holy One, and that the Bible is not nearly as lacking in feminine imagery as we once thought. The Holy Wisdom of God, for example, (the Hagia Sophia) is feminine, and one could add several other examples. Still, an implacably masculine portrait of God remains very dominant, and Jesus was a man, not an androgyne. Vaishnava devotees, however, believe Sri Caitanya was the dual incarnation of both Radha and Krishna. He was at once male and female. In him Krishna transformed himself into Radha, in order, as it were, to experience his own love. Gender lines seem less ineradicable.

This can produce some fascinating results. For example, when I came to Vrndavana, I was told by my hosts that—symbolically—no men were allowed in the town. All residents and guests had to "become" Radha in order to live there, even for a short time, so they could love and worship Krishna. At first I merely smiled at the suggestion. But as the days went by, to my own amazement I actually began to appreciate what it might be like to be a *gopi,* a female devotee. This realization led to a certain loosening of my grip on the fixed gender roles into which most of us are so thoroughly socialized. In some small ways I began to think and feel like a woman, or at least as I imagined a woman might feel. It was both exhilarating and queasy. Perhaps Vaishnavism carries an important theological insight, especially as we discover how arbitrary and impoverishing strict gender allocations can be. I hope that this insight will become an important element in a future Christian-Vaishnava dialogue.

Three years after my visit to Vrndavana, on a fine autumn day, one of the Hindu scholars I had met during my visit there called me up. He had come to America to deliver a guest lecture at a university in California, he told me, but had stopped by to visit Cambridge. Could we talk?

I was glad to see him and to try to reciprocate for the hospitality the sages of Vrndavana had shown me. I took him to the best Indian restaurant in town (called the Gandhi) for a vegetarian feast. As we munched chapatis and curry, I asked him about something I had wondered about off and on ever since I had returned. Did he think that Hinduism in America, and especially his own Vaishnava tradition, would ever mature to the point where a full-blown dialogue would be possible here, so Americans don't have to go to India for it? Or would that be asking too much of a movement that is so young, is still organizing itself, and is still beset with internal divisions and external hostility? I told him that I looked forward to an intellectually sophisticated yet spiritually authentic articulation of his tradition taking root in the West because it would sharpen the challenge to dialogue for Christians who still mistakenly think of Hinduism as something distant and exotic. What did he think?

My guest cooled my ardor somewhat by reminding me politely first of all that his own tradition does not exist to function as the stimulator of a revival of Christianity. He also told me that many Indians—and he included himself among them—viewed the prospects of an Americanized Hinduism with something less than enthusiasm.

"Why," I asked, in all innocence, unable to conceive of how any thoughtful person in any faith tradition could look upon such a development with anything but the keenest anticipation.

"Because," he said, "if it's really Hindu, it won't be American, and if it's really American, it won't be Hindu." He returned to his curry. Apparently he felt that was about all that needed to be said on the subject.

But I persisted. For many years I have been intrigued with the question of how a religious tradition that originates in one culture can move into another without losing its core meaning. Historically, both Buddhism, which started in India, and Christianity, which began in Palestine, have made such transitions successfully. So much so that these faiths are most vigorous in areas outside their lands of origin. Was it not exciting to him, I asked my guest, to see that his own tradition was now making the same move, this time into a modern Western society?

He did not share my sense of excitement. There is in all Indian thought, he reminded me, a strong inbred distrust of any interpretation of any kind in the realm of spiritual knowledge. The suspicion applies both to "reforming" the Hindu tradition in modern urban India and to "interpreting" it to the West. It springs from the Hindu's belief that all spiritual knowledge is eternal, not even partly a product of history and culture. This means it should not be adjusted, either to changing times in India or to different cultures elsewhere. "All change is decadence," he said, as he spooned some saffron rice into his chapati.

By this time I was confused. I could not tell for sure whether my lunch partner was simply quoting his more conservative colleagues or expressing his own views. I told him I thought that I understood the grave risks we run by interpreting our traditions and that this holds for Christians and Hindus alike. But neither should we forget the enormous danger of not interpreting them. Of course, I conceded, there are pitfalls involved in interpreting, whether within one's own culture or in another one, but the danger of not interpreting can be demonstrated by the fossilized remains of religious movements that decided not to try. I felt myself growing eloquent. I told him about the premonition I had had while living in Vrndavana that I might be watching the last gasp of a historic faith, one that was being swamped by modern urban India. Will the Vaishnava sages try to speak to this new culture? Could the experience of their new Hindu coreligionists in America, who started out in Manhattan's Lower East Side, teach them anything about how to do so? Ironically, there has already been a certain rebound effect.

There are already city-dwelling Indians in Bombay and Calcutta who have embraced the Vaishnava tradition (after having been nonreligious) because of their contacts with American devotees. What does the experience of American Hinduism, where some reforms and interpretations have been made (such as allowing women devotees certain privileges), mean for the future of Hinduism in modernizing India?

I grew more animated. I found myself pointing my finger and insisting that a religious tradition that does not interpret itself—to different cultures and to succeeding ages—eventually becomes a dead tradition.

My guest seemed to be scrutinizing the contents of his tea cup. My eloquence seemed to be getting me nowhere. Suddenly, just as an instantaneous moment of insight is said to come to a Zen adept, I saw what I was doing, and why our luncheon dialogue had bogged down. Throughout our conversation I had been relying on an unspoken premise which, although it seems self-evident to Christians, makes no sense to Hindus, namely, that *change* is not only real but good. Furthermore, I had derived from this premise my belief that the message of God can and must be interpreted and reinterpreted to succeeding generations and changing eras and epochs. For the Hindu, or at least for many Hindus, change usually means decline from a more perfect state and is largely illusory in any case. God never changes. We do. Was I trying, perhaps inadvertently, to Christianize this unsuspecting Hindu?

Maybe so, but it also occurred to me that just as Christians have much to learn from Hindus, there might be something they could learn from us as well. For the fact is that much as they are loathe to admit it, many contemporary Hindu thinkers now concede that change, if undesirable, is at least real in some measure. Even Vrndavana—which now has cars and telephones and TV—is not exempt. And India is no longer isolated, if indeed it ever was, from the rest of the world. Could Christians help Hindus learn to interpret?

Of course, there are perils in any interpretive theology. But Christians believe that if God is God, then the message will not be lost or distorted—at least not forever—by human beings. If God wills to speak to all people in all ages and cultures, then God will preserve the integrity of that Word. This means that we can—indeed must—enter into the imposing thicket of interpretation and dialogue (since one always implies the other), perhaps with fear and trembling, but without being afraid we will lose it all. For Christians this willingness to venture is based on the confidence that God's "word" ultimately takes the shape of a human being who is both at home in, and a stranger to, all ages and cultures. There have been followers of Jesus in India since at least the third century C.E., so Jesus was at home in India long before Krishna got to Washington Square Park. Indian Christians have interpreted the faith and even made it Indian, but no one accuses them of diluting it.

After a while I stopped talking while we ate and drank quietly. I was becoming a little embarrassed that I might have trespassed the boundaries of dialogue. But my guest saved the situation. What did I think, he asked. Even if they wanted to, could Hindus ever really root here in this land which has no ancient past? Could they do so with sufficient religious depth and reality to become genuine dialogue partners for American Christians?

He had deftly saved our conversation, so I weighed my words very carefully. There is much faddishness and much that is artificial and superficial, I said, about the current American fascination with Eastern spirituality. In Oriental countries, one hears unpleasant tales of what people call "rice Christians," those who came to the mission to get free rice and who, when the rice ran out, promptly returned to Buddhism or Hinduism. In the West we have the equivalent. But what is being passed out at the Asian mission to America is not rice—it is free (or sometimes not so free) therapy. And the same thing happens: while the psychological goodies are abundant, the disciples keep coming. As long as their affiliation with a particular guru or group is affording an "interesting experience," or fulfilling a need to be different, or providing an outlet for spiritual delectation, they stay. But when the satisfaction of these needs doesn't seem to be continuing in full supply, or the awful arduousness of the new path becomes evident, they drift away. Every American city has its quota of restless and dissatisfied consumers of spirituality who have dashed from one pair of lotus feet to another, sworn eternal fealty, then left when the psychic rice ran out.

My guest suggested that perhaps I should speak with a little more compassion for the people who come to a tradition through this back door. When you are starved, you need rice, and you go where it is available. Conversely, the people who seek out Asian forms of spirituality here in America for what may really be psychological reasons are not by nature evil, gluttonous people. They are taught by a profit-oriented, merchandising culture that consumer commodities provide human fulfillment. They are infected with what the Tibetan Buddhist teacher Chogyam Trungpa calls "spiritual materialism."

I agreed, and I told him the result is that many approach Eastern religious movements like capricious shoppers, pushing their carts from one aisle to another, unable to slake their spiritual gluttony.

He nodded. He said that was exactly what made him skeptical about the long-range staying power of any Asian religious tradition in America.

But I did not want to leave it at that. We also have to recognize, I said, what might be called the "spiritual readiness" of the West to hear the message of Vaishnava Hinduism. The reason is that Americans may now be tiring of the excesses of consumer capitalism. We are becoming aware that our personal values, morality, and perceptions of meaning are all misshaped by the ethos of consumerism and that our most primal energies (fear, love, hope) are wasted on salable items that are alleged to satisfy inner hungers. The advertising industry forges a direct connection between our underlying needs and the things that are supposed to satisfy those needs. Of course they do not. So people are drawn into a value structure that fails to provide real meaning. The end result is a residue of unsatisfied hungers and unresolved fears curdling into rage. I told him that in my opinion at least part of the violence in our society is a result of this frustrated spiritual hunger. People don't succeed as well as they are told they ought to, and they take out that frustration on other people.

He nodded again but asked what this disillusionment had to do with the "spiritual readiness" I had mentioned.

There is, I said, a positive side to this frustration. The consumerist culture elicits a kind of resistance, especially among young people who have begun to emerge from their childhood homes and so are no longer completely defined by familial expectations, but have not as yet locked themselves into career trajectories and mortgages. It is at this turning-point age that many "seekers" are attracted to alternative life-meaning systems. Critics of the "cults" claim that such young people are victims: lonely, vulnerable kids who are picked off the streets and brainwashed. But the truth is that they are potential adults who have not yet been socialized into the values of an accumulating society and are therefore still open to other life patterns. This is why there is a certain spiritual readiness for other traditions, including Hindu ones, in America.

Now my guest astonished me. If this is the case, he asked, why should this spiritual readiness not also be a readiness for Christ? After all, he went on, Jesus did not conform to the career pattern or to the dominant values of his day either. If Christianity were following him, would it not also be providing an alternative to the debased values supplied by the consumer ethos?

This was turning out to be a curious dialogue indeed. Was he making my speech? Unfortunately, I told him, the vast majority of those who call themselves Christians here in America are also caught up in the consumer culture. Still, I said, I agreed with him that the readiness we see in many Americans to turn East also reveals a genuine opportunity for a Christianity that takes Jesus' way of life seriously.

Again my guest astonished me, although knowing what I knew—even then—about his tradition, he should not have. He said he hoped we Christians would seize this new opening. He had no particular stake, he said, in Hinduism or in any one faith. He just wanted these young people to find God. If they did so through Christ, so much the better.

I thought about my curious dialogue with the visitor from Vrndavana for a long time after he had left. He had proved to me despite himself, and in ways I could not have foreseen, that a Hindu tradition thoroughly rooted in America will be salutary for our sometimes lethargic American Christianity. He had done so, ironically, by not making a case for Hinduism at all, but by conceding the field in advance.

I believe we are just at the beginning of a genuine Hindu-Christian dialogue. Bringing the encounter home is bound to help. When a religious movement comes into a new culture, its intensity of devotion is more noticeable and more attractive—in part because the people who make the long journey to another part of the world must, like Swami Prabhupada and Mateo Ricci, have a higher-than-average degree of commitment. Also, the "native" recruits to that movement will display, as new recruits always do, enthusiasm that becomes even more noticeable because it is played off against a complacent cultural background. When a religious tradition has been around for ten, twenty, or thirty generations, it makes significant compromises not only with a culture's good features but with its bad ones as well. Even though from time to time it may give birth to internal revitalization movements, constant cultural accommodation inevitably dilutes its critical power. This is one reason why some Eastern traditions succeed—at least for a time—in the West.

But this dynamic also moves in the other direction. Jesus continues to be very attractive to many people in Asian countries. Millions of Hindus in India have become Christians, in part because—especially if they came from the lower castes—they were looking for an alternative. The Jesuits who traveled to China in the sixteenth century were esteemed by the Chinese as sublime embodiments of wisdom and piety. They immediately became advisers to the emperor. Many more Chinese might have become Christians had the pope not been afraid that the Jesuits were accepting too many aspects of Chinese culture by wearing mandarin robes and integrating Christian theology with Chinese philosophy.

The resident religious tradition anywhere can react in several ways when this outside challenge comes. It can be defensive and propagandize against the newcomers. It can persecute them or throw them out. Or it can view the new arrival as a source of stimulation, renewal, even of grace. The Brahma Samaj movement in India in the nineteenth century took the latter course, constituting at the same time a response to Western Christianity and a much-needed reform movement within Hinduism. Gandhi is a particularly vivid example of one Indian response to Christianity. It is virtually impossible to understand the enormous power of his spirituality without seeing him as a man who, while remaining in the Hindu tradition, was also drawn to Jesus and the Sermon on the Mount. Conversely, Martin Luther King, Jr., a Christian, was deeply influenced by the Hindu Gandhi. Without resorting to mindless syncretism, contact with another faith can help me uncover other dimensions of my own.

It has now been several years since I rode down Fifth Avenue with Krishna. Since then, the Hare Krishna movement has fallen on difficult times, not only because of the loss of its founder and the bitter divisions that ensued, but also because of the continued legal harassment its members have been subjected to. I view this decline with sadness because it postpones the global interaction of religions that the Festival of Chariots once made so dramatically visible. While I may have my doubts about many facets of the Hindu tradition, I suspect God has some purpose in creating the new opportunities for dialogue our shrunken globe makes possible and requires. I look forward to the conversation. I have learned—in part from Shrivatsa Goswami and his colleagues in Vrndavana—to have confidence that God's truth vastly exceeds the truth any single tradition can convey and that it is God's truth that will eventually prevail.

4
Buddhists and Christians

The bell began ringing in my dream, a sweet, unintrusive pealing, distant and melodious. But as the dream faded I knew that the bell was sounding just outside my window, that Brother Richard in his plaid jacket and Levi's was pulling the cord, and that in ten minutes, at 4:30 A.M., the monks would be gathering for matins:

> O sing unto the Lord a new song:
> Sing unto the Lord, all the earth.
> Sing unto the Lord, bless his name;
> Show forth his salvation from day to day.

Without allowing myself the time to decide whether I wanted to get up or not, I rolled out of bed, sloshed cold water from the basin on my face, and pulled on my clothes. My visitor's cell in the Weston priory, following the explicit directions of Saint Benedict's Rule itself, was scantily but adequately furnished with a cot, chair, table, lamp, closet, sink, and crucifix—little to distract. It was February in Vermont and cold. I put on heavy socks and a wool sweater and picked my way downstairs to the simple common room where the earliest prayers of the day would be sung.

When I got to the room, most of the tiny monastery's sixteen monks were already there, sitting quietly on cushions in a semicircle near the huge picture window. Along the edge of the darkened hills across a valley, the gray light of the new day was just beginning to appear. Now one monk struck a chord on his guitar. Together they all sang, in perfect harmony, to a modern tune:

> Calm is the night, O Lord
> as we wait for you.
> All the stars are laughing
> at our wonder.

For a moment I felt utterly at home—with myself, with the monks, and with the universe. For a millennium and a half, Benedictine monks have been greeting the morning with songs of praise. Here a steel-string guitar, Zen-type cushions, and a melody reminiscent of Judy Collins had been added to an ancient ritual with no apparent incongruence. After the prayers and psalms, we returned to our cells for a period of individual prayer, then gathered for a silent breakfast, then proceeded to the work of the day. Underfoot the snow squeaked in the twenty-below temperature.

I was visiting a Benedictine monastery because, as is the case with many people, my encounter with Oriental spirituality had aroused my interest in a part of my own tradition I had previously overlooked. It was odd to have lived in a Buddhist monastery before I even visited a Christian one. But after trying the Tibetan Buddhist discipline off and on for three years it finally became evident to me that it just wasn't taking. So I asked my Buddhist teacher what to do, and he suggested I try a Christian monastery. So I did. But it was no accident that I had chosen this kind of Christian monastery. The Tibetans are, in some sense, the Benedictines of Buddhism. Although serious in their monastic life, the Tibetans have not shunned the world as many Theravada Buddhists and some Trappists and Carthusians have. Their monasteries performed in Tibet the same civilizing function the Benedictines performed in Barbarian Europe. Although both Tibetan (Vajrayana) Buddhists and Benedictines recognize that not everyone can or should be a monk, their communal discipline is a way to live together in the world, not a way to abandon it. So here I was, a Baptist sitting on a Zen cushion in a Benedictine monastery on the advice of a Tibetan lama.

Among the reasons why people turn East today is that they are looking for friendship, for experience, and for a teacher and a teaching that rings true. In Buddhist language, they are looking for a *sangha* (a group of serious colleagues), a guru (a teacher), and a dharma (an authoritative teaching). The question that inevitably presented itself to my mind when I returned from Naropa was whether any or all of these might be found in Christianity itself. As I lived among the monks during those days in Vermont, I thought a lot about *sangha,* guru, and dharma—and about their possible counterparts in my own tradition.

At first glance, parallels seem all too obvious. The search for *sangha* recalls the biblical idea of the covenant people, the congregation or the *ecclesia.* Dharma suggests a comparison with the gospel. The place of Jesus, at first, seems similar to that of a guru. The question remains, however, whether there is real similarity below the surface.

Sangha *and Friendship*

Biblical faith recognizes the universal human need for friendship. In the Genesis narrative, God creates men and women to live in friendship and mutuality, not in isolation. But fear and possessiveness lead to betrayal, fratricide, and exile. The Adam and Eve and the Cain and Abel in each of us destroy mutuality through jealousy and hunger for power: the result is loneliness and suspicion. But it does not end there. In the biblical saga, "God" is that nameless energy that pulls isolated people out of loneliness and oppression into a new form of human solidarity. God is disclosed primarily as the one who creates a nation out of scattered tribes, makes a covenant (*berith*) with them, and promises that eventually the covenant will include all the peoples of the earth.

The most significant feature of the new community that God initiates among the separated tribes is that it not only binds people to each other but binds them at the same time to God. The importance of this idea of covenant should not be lost sight of just because it is cast in mythological language. The inner meaning of "covenant" is that the most basic power of the universe is itself a source of, and a participant in, human friendship. Friendship is not something human beings must eke out of the wilderness themselves. Friendship includes the constellations and the oceans and the source from which they all arise. *Berith* is no mere social contract. God enters into friendship with the world and with humanity. The covenant is not an incidental aspect of God. It expresses the divine essence. God is that which makes friendship possible in human life.

The concept of *berith* gives the idea of friendship a centrality in biblical faith that goes beyond even the notion of *sangha*. Since the inner mystery of the cosmos is both the originator of and a partner in the covenant, the divine presence within each person becomes the basis for friendship. This community is not based on mere consensus or shared aspiration. Nor is it hierarchical. Since all human rank and station shrink to insignificance before God, all members of the covenant are essentially equal. Leadership and authority are intended only to serve the community. Moreover, the basis of human participation in the community is affected by the nature of *berith*. People can accept and live in the community freely because they have not created it themselves. It is not some awkward arrangement that constantly needs to be mended or pumped up. In a community with such a grounding, people can let each other be. Since everyone in the community enjoys the same status, there is a quality of freedom that no mutual interest society can have.

This all sounds good theologically, but it does not answer the question of why Westerners are looking for friendship in Oriental forms. What has happened to covenant community in the West? Like any expression of friendship, the reality of the covenant has been damaged by the acids of the modern industrial world. Eventually, these corrosions will surely take their toll of neo-Oriental *sanghas* as well. But there were flaws in the way the covenant worked even before it was attacked by industrial values. In actual practice, the covenant community, despite its cosmic grounding, never fully broke out of its ethnic definition. Although here and there in Jewish theology the idea of an inclusive human community is expressed, it is usually in visionary or utopian terms. In reality, the covenant was mostly for Israelites.

The problem was not solved by the advent of Christianity. At first, the Christian movement gave the covenant a universal quality, at least theoretically. In the great debate at the Council of Jerusalem, it was decided that uncircumcised gentiles could also be full members of the *ecclesia*, the new community founded by Christ and intended to appeal to everyone regardless of lineage. Christianity began as a movement of hundreds of tiny "societies of friends" spread around the shores of the Mediterranean and tied to each other at first only through visiting teachers and the exchange of letters and gifts. But it soon became hierarchical and exclusive. Finally, when the emperor Constantine made the new faith the ideology of his empire and entire Visigoth tribes were baptized en masse, being a Christian meant joining an organization and adhering to a prescribed creed. The societies of friends soon virtually disappeared.

The early Benedictines made one response to this disappearance. It is often said that the monastic movement began in the West because thousands of individuals became disgusted with the church's subservience to the empire and with the widespread corruption that accompanied its legal establishment. One may argue, however, that people abandoned imperial religion and lived in monastic settlements to reestablish a measure of communalism. They fled to the desert not to escape the despoiling of doctrine but to get away from the destruction of circles of friends and their replacement by a hierarchically ordered imperium. Christianity seems to have introduced the dream of a network of local communities united in a universal covenant—only to have lost it almost immediately.

But the idea of a covenant community was never entirely lost. Parallel to the official history of the church from Constantine on, there is another history of the restless search for a viable form of community in which friendship could flourish. Bands of hermits, roving groups of monks, heretical movements, and religious orders kept appearing. In almost every one of them, the idea of spiritual friendship and sharing was central. It was the heart of the teaching of Saint Benedict, who lived in the early sixth century. People took great risks and endured awful deprivation in these movements. During the five-hundred-year period from 1200 C.E. until 1700 C.E. in which the events we call the Reformation took place, thousands of efforts were made, most of them short lived, to reconstitute the *ecclesia* on a more communal, less hierarchical basis. It would be tempting to reread the tempestuous history of Christianity not so much as strife over doctrines as a series of attempts to establish an authentic community. The labels used by the various parties during the Reformation help to show what was at stake: "papist," "Congregationalist," and "Presbyterian" refer to different theories of how a community is best organized, nurtured, and governed. Christians, too, have spent a lot of energy in the search for *sangha.*

After 1600, the American wilderness received thousands of settlers who crossed the seas determined to found religious communities in which fraternity and sorority would flourish. They often failed, but throughout the nineteenth century the United States was dotted with religious communes and spiritual utopias—in Ephrata, Oneida, New Harmony, the Shaker villages, to name only some of the better-known examples. I believe we can see in the current search for *sangha,* which has brought thousands of Americans to the doors of neo-Oriental groups, a continuing expression of a quest that began millennia ago and that has had an especially lively history in America.

Dharma and Gospel

With respect to dharma, or teaching, one thing seems clear. Many of the people who "turn East" are searching for a discipline that will enable them to meet both the sacred and the secular aspects of life with a directness not gutted by abstraction or sullied by analysis. Their quest represents the revolt of heart against head, which is also familiar to students of revivalism in Christianity. It is important to repeat, however, that for many such searchers this quest for immediacy is not directed only at the experience of God. It is a search for an unaffected and honest encounter with all one meets—with nature, other people, and the self. Although some Eastern movements claim that the techniques they teach can produce a direct relationship with the holy, others explicitly deny that they can do any such thing. What such disciplines do make possible for many people is a way of coming into touch with persons and things without having to see them through a fuzzy screen of cerebral overlay.

Where does the screen come from? Here Christian and Oriental answers differ. I heard Ram Dass, the psychologist-turned-guru, articulate a typical Eastern answer to a large audience of enthusiastic listeners some time ago. Like many other neo-Oriental teachers, Ram Dass located the distorting screen in the phenomenon of language. He told of the problem he had eating pizza, an activity sure to bridge the gap to his youthful audience. Ram Dass said that in times past, just as he was about to bite into a large onion, mushroom, and cheese pizza, he often heard a voice within him say, "Eating pizza." The voice was not judgmental or mocking, just observing. Yet putting the experience of eating pizza into words while it was happening detracted from the sheer taste of the pungent ingredients.

So far, I can agree completely with the diagnosis. All of us seem to have as a constant companion this loquacious little interior commentator, editorialist, and observer. His running chatter constantly distracts us from the pure taste, smell, and feel of whatever it is we are doing. Reality becomes increasingly hidden behind its labels. Small talk can be distracting, which is why the Benedictines eat their meals in silence and the Trappists discourage any idle chit-chat. How do we get beyond labels?

In Buddhist thought, the word *dharmakaya* is sometimes used to designate the raw experience of being. It stands for the sheer "thatness" of reality, what is there before we name it or classify it. It is the pizza in the mouth at the moment when tongue and saliva and onions and hot tomato sauce seem indistinguishable from each other. *Dharmakaya* might also be described as the way of touching and seeing that the discipline of sitting meditation exemplifies. When one is simply watching one's own breath, no words or concepts are needed. But not all experiences are as pleasant as eating pizza, so meditation should not be presented as a technique to make life happier. Only a saccharine form of meditation would produce exclusively enjoyable results. One who can taste pizza directly will inevitably go on to be able to taste anger, fear, and pain more keenly also. That is why the experience of *dharmakaya* needs to be placed in a more inclusive vision of the world. It requires both a community of support, which in some forms of Buddhism is provided by the *sangha,* and an ethical framework, which Mahayana Buddhism supplies for many people in the ideal of bodhisattva (the notion that one does not accept the fullness of human liberation oneself until all sentient creatures share it).

In order to understand how the message of Jesus compares with the idea of *dharmakaya,* one must begin by noting that the gospel is not a "message" in the usual sense at all. Jesus himself is the message. The gospel is neither a dogma about him nor even a compilation of his own teachings. The reason the Jesus dharma centers in the life of a concrete historical person rather than in a body of verbal teachings derives from an insight that is not altogether unlike the notion of *dharmakaya.* The reason goes back to the ancient Hebrew recognition that no one can adequately represent either God or human beings in words or pictures. According to the Second Commandment, one should never use any image to depict either God or human beings or animals, and, according to ancient Hebrew custom, the name of God should never be uttered by human lips. All these proscriptions express the belief that, since God is not just a transcendent being but the essential constituent in the being of everything, there is something in every person and thing that resists labels. We err badly, this teaching insists, if we believe that what is real in the world around us can be grasped by words and concepts. We are commanded to make no images, not because it would be disrespectful, but because no image, no matter how carefully wrought, can possibly do justice to that which it is supposed to depict. All such constructs inevitably mislead and distort.

There are differences, however, between the Buddhist idea of *dharmakaya,* with its suspicion of words, and the biblical idea of the Holy, with its suspicion of trying to depict either God or human beings in any way. The difference is that, while in most Buddhist schools of thought it is the words themselves that distort, in biblical faith it is not the words but our human inclination to use words to twist reality in our direction. Words themselves, and even pictures, are not, in the biblical view, essentially evil or misleading. But because we live as human persons in a world infected by possessiveness and hostility, we inevitably tend to use even the most valuable gifts in destructive ways. The problem is not language or concepts as such but rather our misuse of them. Adam and Eve spoke with each other in the innocence of Eden. We lose our capacity for *dharmakaya* or direct experience (symbolized by the Garden of Eden), not because we use concepts and language, but because we try to control and dominate, seize and grasp. It is not the use of words that poisons our interaction with life; rather, our prior poisoning of life in turn poisons our words and concepts.

Since the Buddhist and biblical views of the locus of the infection differ, naturally their prescriptions for recovery vary too. Since in the biblical view our basic dislocation is a fractured relationship to the people and things around us, only the healing of these relationships will allow us to begin to use words to affirm people rather than to control them. The biblical faith teaches that this healing and restoring energy is available and that, as we are touched by it, our thinking and speaking become less despoiling. For Buddhists, one slowly learns to realize that all the words and categories we use are illusory constructs, and this insight is itself liberating. In the Buddhist view, we learn to use words sparingly because there is no way words can avoid distorting: "Words are liars." In the biblical view, we allow ourselves to be weaned away from our need to grasp and clutch at those around us, and we find that this allows us to see and speak with less distortion—even to say, "I love you," not to control someone but because we mean it.

Both Buddhism and biblical faith recognize the validity of the human need for a direct encounter with the real stuff of life. Buddhism locates our alienation from reality in ignorance, wishful thinking, abstracting, concept pandering. It has elaborated a sophisticated range of techniques and teachings for helping people to rise above this ignorance and face reality as it is. Biblical faith attributes our dilemma not to ignorance but to fear and lovelessness, our anxious need either to dominate the people around us or to keep them at a safe distance. Therefore, the Buddhist path emphasizes overcoming ignorance, and the biblical course concentrates on the restoration of mutuality.

Both the overlapping and the distinction between these two interpretations of a universal malady come to focus in the practice of meditation. Some Buddhists claim that, the more they meditate, the surer they become of the illusory quality of relationships. In my own experience of meditation, quite the opposite occurs: I become increasingly aware that my life is constituted by relationships and that the health of those relationships is largely a matter of how much I am falling into controlling and allowing myself to be controlled by the people around me. When I return time and again to my departing breath, it is like taking a step away from the need to master or to be mastered and a step toward the kind of mutuality that is possible when the liberating ingredients of any relationship are permitted to surface. When I get up from the cushion, my feeling toward other people is both more independent and more interdependent, closer and not as cloying, more integral and less entangling.

I agree with the Buddhist teaching that meditation helps people respond to "what is really there." But included in what is really there is something that moves toward me from others, an energy that enables human beings to take a step beyond gamesmanship, toward meeting. This energy has its source not just in human beings themselves but in something embedded in the structure of the cosmos. If I had to call it something, I would use the word "grace." It is the mystery of grace that has the power to soften our hearts, still our fears, and restore us to each other. As this process begins, the poison level in our language goes down, concepts begin to function as bridges instead of walls, and one can accept people as God accepts them—not for what they can or cannot do for us but for what they are. A kind of *dharmakaya* occurs. Finally, we may be able to nibble a pizza without a troublesome little internal commentator whispering in our ear.

The Christian gospel is a kind of dharma, a teaching. What it says, however, is that a direct encounter, a *dharmakaya,* not only with God but with our fellow earthlings, with nature and with our own deepest selves, *is* in fact possible. The "message" comes, however, not as advice or exhortation. It comes in the only way it is credible, in a human person, Jesus, who actually did all these things and who points us toward other human beings as the indispensable clue to the discovery of the daily *dharmakaya* in our midst.

Jesus and the Guru

Jesus himself is the centerpiece of the Christian dharma. Was he then also a guru? Ever since he first appeared preaching and healing in the remote province of Galilee, people have tried to find the right word for Jesus, a credible way of grasping what he was about. In the pages of the New Testament alone, dozens of attempts to name and classify him appear. One group of followers, fired by a passion for the liberation of Judea from Rome, wanted him to be King of the Judeans, or the "Son of David," the one who would restore the storied empire of King David. Others wanted him to bring back religious purity to the Jews, to cleanse and purge and sanctify the nation. To these spiritual revivalists, Jesus seemed anointed by God in much the same way the great prophets and John the Baptist had been. Still others hoped this unlikely Galilean would actually become the legendary Son of Man mentioned widely in the popular piety of the day, a cosmic hero who would close the present world age with a crash and introduce a universal epoch of justice and peace, punishing the wicked and rewarding the righteous.

Jesus disappointed all of them. Occasionally, he seemed to lend hope to the national liberation enthusiasts. They must have been sparked with anticipation, for example, when he entered Jerusalem in a kind of caricature of the great Roman triumphal marches, riding a colt, with the crowds strewing branches before him. Still, he led no attack on the occupation forces and discouraged his followers from carrying weapons. Although he was finally executed in a manner clearly reserved for insurrectionaries, this happened because the local Judean leadership clique was obviously upset by his presence and succeeded in persuading the Romans that he was a menace.

But Jesus burst the hopes of the other groups, too. Those who looked for a great revival and a restoration of religious purity were enraged by his violation of ritual taboos. He would not engage in ceremonial hand washing, and he healed people on the Sabbath, which, though condoned by other rabbis of his time, infuriated the stricter interpreters of seventh-day propriety. As if this were not enough, he completely dashed the hopes of the religious-revival party by associating with the ritually unclean—lepers and gentiles—and by insisting that such pariahs would actually precede the righteous people into the Kingdom of God. He especially confused and disillusioned the people who wanted to apply to him the title Son of Man, which was the name attached to the coming hero of the popular folk religion of his day. He did this first by accepting the title, then allowing himself to be defeated, humiliated, and killed, the exact opposite of the Son of Man scenario.

Jesus seemed determined to smash every expectation, label, and title anyone tried to affix to him. He destroyed some by refusing the title in the first place. He destroyed others by accepting the title (Messiah, Son of Man, maybe even King of the Judeans) and then acting in a way that exploded what the title meant to those who used it.

Jesus would not be what anyone wanted him to be or do what they wanted him to do. Although he healed and taught and even fed people at times, he was not really a healer or teacher in the usual sense. When he cured people, it was to demonstrate the healing powers of the new epoch he claimed was dawning. When he taught, it was not to convey a tradition or pass on some kind of wisdom. Rather than teaching in the normal sense of the word, Jesus announced something. He pointed people to a spiritual reality he called the reign of God, which he insisted was now accessible to everyone and did not have to be awaited or anticipated in some near or remote future.

Jesus left behind him a trail of shattered illusions and wrecked expectations. When we say today that Jesus was in some way a key clue to the nature of God, this expectation-destroying quality of his life suggests what such a claim means. The God Jesus discloses will not be the God anyone wants. This God will not be a mere extension of human programs and aspirations. Divine "transcendence," therefore, is not a matter of spatial distance or mystic fuzziness. It refers to the continuous power of the Holy to break through all concepts, doctrines, mental sets, and cultural patterns. Jesus reveals God exactly because he was not what anybody expected or wanted. He refused to be classified, and he constantly forced people to deal directly with him rather than with their ideas about him. In doing so, Jesus exemplified in his life something Buddhist teachers constantly emphasize—that reality is always different from even our best ways of talking and thinking about it.

People's efforts to cast Jesus in a role that would serve their own purposes continued after his death. Even the pages of the New Testament are not entirely free of this redrawing of Jesus' portrait. Within a few years, he was depicted as a dying and rising nature god in the style of Mithras. Later, he became a frowning and all-powerful Byzantine emperor, the Pantocrator, and still later a gentle teacher of virtue and charity, as the nineteenth-century liberals saw him. It is understandable that people over the centuries have tried to grasp the meaning of Jesus in categories familiar to them. Since Jesus cannot be entirely defined by any single role, this process will always go on. Each attempt has its own strengths and its own dangers. So today we find Jesus pictured as a circus clown, a national liberation rebel, a teacher of mystical wisdom, a preacher of feminism, an impulsive superstar, or, as Kazantzakis portrays him, a hot-blooded romantic hero. But because the spirit of Christ is still alive, the same refusal to be pigeonholed goes on today. No one of these costumes ever quite fits. Jesus still continues to shatter expectations and smear the pictures people paint of him.

Today, as the turn East proceeds apace, there are two titles drawn from Eastern thought that some people are eager to press on Jesus. Both carry with them a considerable weight of Oriental metaphysics and theology, but, once again, neither quite fits the one to whom they wish to attach it. One of these titles is "avatar." The other is "guru."

An avatar, the conception of which originated in Hindu spirituality, is one among many embodiments of the ultimate. Ideas of what an avatar is vary widely, but one current theory teaches that in each age there is an avatar on the earth somewhere—that Confucius, Moses, Jesus, the Buddha, Saint Francis, Muhammad, Lao Tzu, and many others were such embodiments of the divine. After these familiar names, the list of candidates begins to vary, depending on who makes the list, but the idea is clear: there is always a divine incarnation walking around on earth somewhere, and, if we are tuned in properly, we can locate him or her.

Although Jesus was probably not familiar with the avatar theory in this form, paradoxically he both abolished it and accepted it at the same time. He abolished the avatar idea, ironically, by accepting it so radically and so universally that it no longer made sense. He did this by allowing himself to be called Christ (or Messiah, which is the same word). In his time, the title meant one who is anointed by God, a special representative of God among others—an idea not unlike that of avatar. However, Jesus went on to insist that, henceforth, God could be found not just in prophets, wise men, or holy teachers but in all human beings. He emphasized the sweeping inclusiveness of "all" by especially singling out the poor, prisoners, sick and disreputable people, the ritually impure, and the racially excluded as the ones in whom the presence of the Holy now dwelled. Jesus was the avatar to end all avatars. If we take his life message seriously, we need not rack our brains to figure out which of the current contenders is an avatar of the divine. All are, and none is. The avatar we are seeking is already in the midst of us, in us and in those closest to us and farthest away.

If Jesus does not quite fit the classical role of avatar, then can he be understood as a guru? The term "guru" is also not one about which there is complete agreement. According to the informative section on the guru-disciple relationship in Herbert V. Guenther and Chogyam Trungpa's *The Dawn of Tantra,* "The term *guru* is a Indian word, which has now almost become part of the English language. Properly used, this term does not refer so much to a human person as to the object of a shift in attention which takes place from the human person who imparts the teaching to the teaching itself. The human person might more properly be called the *kalyanamitra* or spiritual friend . . . one who is able to impart spiritual guidance because he has been through the process himself."

The writers go on to say that, although at a certain stage in the teaching process the guru may be identified with the *kalyanamitra,* this should not become a matter of personality cult. Eventually, the teaching eclipses the teacher. Finally, the world itself, as it unfolds from moment to moment, becomes the guru.

Can we see Jesus either as a guru or as a *kalyanamitra?* Soon after the death of Jesus, a movement began among the first-century Greek-speaking followers of the new Christian movement that understood him as what scholars now call a *theios aner* (divine man). These early Hellenistic Christians saw Jesus as a superhuman figure, endowed with near magical powers, the possessor of a kind of supernatural knowledge that he selectively reveals as divine revelation to those of his own choosing. The majority of early Christians, however, rejected the divine man theology. It seems clear that one of the main purposes Saint Mark had in mind when he wrote his account of the life of Jesus, the earliest gospel we have, was to fight this first-century effort to make Jesus into the equivalent of a guru in our present popular sense.

According to Saint Mark and the writers of the other synoptic Gospels, Jesus was decidedly not a teacher of divine wisdom who selectively imparted a secret teaching to a specially chosen few. He healed the sick and was reported to have worked other miracles. But nothing he did of this nature was calculated to dazzle audiences. On the contrary, rather than using his gifts to attract attention, Jesus often warned people not to make too much of the healings themselves. Above all, Jesus did not hand down clandestine lore. When he spoke, he addressed crowds in the open fields and in the synagogues. His whole life was devoted to warning people against teachings that were reserved for the select few or that required some rare gift of spiritual receptivity. He claimed that even the despised collectors of the Roman taxes could understand, and he seemed to go out of his way to consort with those he called the "poor in spirit," the religiously inept and the morally retarded. If we think of the title "guru," not in the elevated sense in which Guenther and Trungpa define it, but in its current popular usage as designating a superlatively holy person, perhaps capable of breathtaking feats, who secretly passes on some supreme wisdom to a selected coterie, then Jesus was no guru.

But can we understand Jesus as a guru in the more refined sense or possibly as a *kalyanamitra,* an experienced spiritual friend? Certainly, if the term "guru" entails a shift of attention from the person to the teaching, Jesus does not qualify. In what still appears to many people as patent arrogance, Jesus insisted that he himself exemplified his own teachings, that the two were inseparable. People eventually had to deal with *him,* not with what he said or with what was said about him.

Is this arrogance? I think not. It is simply Jesus' way of forcing us to deal directly with people rather than with ideas or conceptualizations. This is why Christianity has been correct in emphasizing that the gospel points to a person, not to a system of thought or an ethical code. Jesus is a "spiritual friend" only insofar as he does what only a very close friend can do: he refuses to allow us to use him to reinforce our habitual patterns and our tendency to throw off the responsibility for our own lives onto other people. He did not permit himself to become the occasion for illusory hopes or passing the buck. He showed the anti-Roman guerrillas that if they believed God would cast off the Roman yoke they were deluding themselves. They would have to bring down the tyrant themselves. Jesus would not cater to the religious hopes of the people who yearned for a spiritual renaissance. He would not allow anyone to cope with him by using platitudes, conventional formulations, or any existing modus operandi. Jesus was a unique person, and as such he enables us to see the uniqueness of all persons.

Jesus is the person par excellence. In him we meet what we then realize is equally true for all persons: they are singular and unrepeatable centers of creativity and decision. They are not merely the occasions for perpetuating our own schemes or illustrations of our ideas or facilities for advancing our programs. Christian theology has correctly insisted that Jesus was both "true God and true man," not some well-blended admixture. He was fully divine and fully human. But in its one-sided reiteration of the "true God" part of this teaching, theology has frequently neglected to say that Jesus also shows us what a true human being is. This side is not only equally important; it is also integral to the "true God" part. No one knows what the "true God" side means unless he knows what the "true person" side means. Jesus is divine *because* he was fully human, and that which is most human in anyone is at the same time the *imago dei,* that which is most divine.

Jesus' final confrontation with the effort of his contemporaries to cast him in the role of guru or *kalyanamitra* came with his decision to allow himself to be identified with God—and then to be crucified. This was the ultimate overturning of dogmas and expectations. Whatever else gods do, they do not allow themselves to be cornered, railroaded, disgraced, and lynched. Jesus had a clear choice. He could have refused the divine title, in which case his crucifixion would have offended no one. Rebels and rabble-rousers of his time frequently met such an end. Or Jesus could have accepted the title and then done what everyone expected God to do: destroy the oppressors, purify the nation, and bring in an era of kindness and goodwill. Either of these courses would have made sense to his contemporaries.

Instead, Jesus chose a third course. He accepted the divine title *and* he allowed himself to be tracked down, tried, and executed. The final destruction of everybody's fondest religious ideas occurred: God on a cross. In this denouement,

Jesus put an end to any notion of God as the great guru in the skies, the magical deus ex machina or the omnipotent Big Brother. As Dietrich Bonhoeffer puts it in one of his most eloquent passages, "The only God who can help us is the one who cannot help."

After nearly two thousand years, the truth about Jesus has still hardly sunk in. Right after his death, stories began to circulate that he had escaped the gibbet, that a look-alike had been substituted, that while the crucifixion occurred he was standing on a nearby hill chuckling. Since then other people have tried to use the resurrection appearances of Jesus to reinstate the idea of a "big daddy" God who solves our problems for us and keeps us in eternal early adolescence. But the resurrection stories depict a crucified figure who still bears the wounds of the nails and who gets hungry and must be fed. True, some current theologians object to this interpretation and argue that a crucified God cannot bring hope to the downtrodden and disenfranchised. Only an omnipotent God, they say, can buoy up the powerless. But Jesus knew better. To the landless peons of his day his life had an unmistakable message: God does not support the rich and the powerful, but neither does he intercede with magic arrows or well-aimed thunderbolts to remove an oppressor from the palace. God liberates the oppressed by enabling them to liberate themselves. This, I believe, is the only credible "liberation theology." Anything else feeds the kind of millennial fantasies that have kept the poor in bondage for centuries.

Was Jesus a guru? Is he a guru? The answer is that whatever kind of guru one is looking for is the one Jesus refuses to be. He is an elusive figure, the saboteur of prefabrications, the true *kalyanamitra* who deftly places the ball back in our court. He is not the guru we want, but he is the guru whom, whether we know it or not, we need.

The monks at Weston Priory go to bed early. Since the day begins at 4:30 A.M. with Brother Richard pulling the bell cord, they need to. Also, the February nights in Vermont are dark and cold. Despite the arctic temperature, I took a walk the night before I left. The frosted air burned my nostrils, and even the stars seemed to shiver. The monastery's dogs barked briefly as I crunched by, but then quickly crept back into their boxes. I felt cold, but comfortable. I was not either a Buddhist or a Benedictine. But I was beginning to see why my Tibetan teacher had sent me here. Through the lens of these monks' life together I had been able to catch a glimpse of something that was mine, something that in its own way could meet the need for *sangha,* dharma, and guru that I had found not only in other people but in myself. I could see that, at least for me, Christian faith, despite the distortions that have marred it, can still answer the universal human yearning for friendship, authentic experience, and trustworthy authority. The canny Tibetan lama who had sent a Baptist seeker to a Benedictine abbey had apparently known exactly what he was doing. In fact, the next morning when the early bell sounded, before I opened my eyes I thought I saw him, my Buddhist teacher, in a fading dream. And like so many statues of the Buddha I have seen, he was smiling.

5

Rabbi Yeshua ben Joseph

It happened during a long ride in a battered orange minibus from Jerusalem up to the Galilee: I discovered that the dialogue between Jews and Christians had entered a whole new phase. I was making my first visit to Israel, and I had arrived alone and unannounced. After years of reading and hearing stories and songs about what I was taught to call "the Holy Land," I had finally decided to see it for myself, not as a guest scholar or visiting lecturer but as a pilgrim. I reveled in the marvelous anonymity. No one met me at the airport. No one in the decrepit old hotel I stayed at inside the old city knew, or cared, who I was. For three days I had explored old Jerusalem and its environs on foot. I stood on the Mount of Olives, attempting to ignore the local children who were trying to sell trinkets and souvenirs. I walked slowly around the circumference of the entire old walled city. I watched, first with amusement and then with revulsion, as the clerical guardians of the Holy Sepulcher, representing rival Christian factions, bickered with each other. I stood quietly near the Wailing Wall while a family who had flown in from New

York celebrated their son's bar mitzvah on the site of Solomon's temple, now within a few steps of the Dome of the Rock and the Mosque of Al-Aqsa.

But Jerusalem is a jittery place, and it does not take long for a visitor to realize that the traditional interpretation of its name as "city of peace" is an empirical as well as an etymological error. (It really means "place of Shalem," the local pre-Israelite deity.) But Jerusalem is not serene. Israelis, Arabs, and foreign tourists brush each other in its narrow alleys but often avoid eye contact. It is a layered city, with strata dating back to before ancient times and piled with deposits from the biblical period, the Roman Empire, the Muslim Caliphate, the Crusaders' Kingdom, the Turkish Empire, the British Mandate, and the new Jewish state of Israel. But despite the confusion and the blatant modernity that often leap out unexpectedly from a movie poster or an ear-splitting transistor, nothing can completely eradicate the aura. I know that Muslims also revere it as their third holiest city, and I look forward to the day when the access of the children of all three of the Abrahamic faiths is settled for good. But for me Jerusalem is the city of David, Solomon, the prophets, and Ezra. And, of course, it is the city where Jesus came to celebrate Passover and where he taught, was betrayed, and met his earthly end. Obviously it was not a particularly peaceful city then either.

In keeping with the edgy atmosphere, my visit to Jerusalem was also not a fully serene one. Whatever tranquillity there might have been was shattered on the third evening when I ran into another American visitor at a shop where I was buying extra film. He wore a yellow sports jacket, sharply pressed slacks, and mirrored sunglasses, and, when he heard me speak English to the proprietor, he introduced himself to me as an independent Christian evangelist. He had come to

Jerusalem, he said, to make contact with those Israelis who were looking forward to the rebuilding of the Temple and the reinstitution of the animal sacrifices that had ended when Herod's temple was destroyed by the Romans in 70 C.E.

At first I was incredulous and asked him quite innocently why anyone would want to do such a bizarre thing. Then it was his turn to be incredulous. Surely I knew, he said with his brow furrowing, that the Book of Daniel and the Book of Revelation both clearly predicted the rebuilding of the Temple as one of the sure signs that we were entering the Last Days. After the reconstruction, he assured me—in tones that somehow combined both a conspiratorial breathiness and an anyone-should-know-this rebuke—the sacrifices of calves and sheep and pigeons would resume. Why, there were Jews, from the ancient priestly line, who even now, he said, were perfecting the nearly forgotten sacrificial techniques. After all these preliminary steps, he added, referring quickly to a jumble of texts from the prophetic and apocalyptic parts of Scripture, an evil empire would attack Israel, which would then be abandoned by its erstwhile but cowardly allies. Then, just when everything looked dark and hopeless, there would be a titanic battle at Armageddon, and God would intervene on Israel's behalf by sending Christ himself to lead the forces of righteousness. Christ would win, of course, whereupon all Jews everywhere would recognize that the Messiah they have awaited for so long was none other than Jesus Christ himself. The Jews would be converted en masse, and thousands of them would then encircle the globe as powerful evangelists winning the lost to Christ.

I was appalled. A strange impulse to reach out and strangle my new unsought acquaintance rose in me, then subsided. Then I wanted to argue. I wanted to try as hard as I could to prove to him that the texts he so craftily recited out of context and inserted into his phantasmagoric end-time scenario had to do with events that had already occurred millennia ago, that they were not predictions about our time. I had heard comparable interpretations before, and I knew that they sprang from that unlikely fusion of biblical literalism, holiness perfectionism, and the occult that we now call "dispensationalist fundamentalism." I remembered that the Scofield Reference Bible I was awarded as a boy for perfect Sunday School attendance advanced one form of these theories in elaborate footnotes and paragraph headings. I even knew that this fatalistic theology of history had been widely popularized in America a decade ago by Hal Lindsey's best-seller *The Late Great Planet Earth*. Lindsey is hardly subtle: "There remains but one more event to completely set the stage for Israel's part in the last great act of her historical drama. This is to rebuild the ancient Temple of worship upon its old site. There is only one place that this Temple can be built, according to the law of Moses. This is upon Mt. Moriah. It is there that the two previous Temples were built." These are Lindsey's words, and even printed on the page of a paperback they had seemed grotesque to me—grotesque, but not ominous. This, however, was something different. Here was a walking-and-talking advocate of Armageddon theology declaiming his fantasy within sight of the Temple Mount itself.

Suddenly I found myself speechless. I could not argue or even prolong the conversation. I just wanted to get away from my self-appointed eschatology instructor as soon as I could, so I made up an excuse and scurried away. But my brief encounter with him had taught me something: whether I liked it or not, a certain type of Jewish-Christian dialogue was already going on. And I desperately wished it were not. I quietly prayed that this charlatan might not meet or talk to too many Israelis or Jews, but I know there were many like him. The euphoria I had felt about being in the Holy City was dashed, so I decided to cheer myself up by purchasing a ticket for a three-day bus tour to the Galilee.

Next morning, I reported early to the bus terminal. Already things looked better. Having now savored the city where Jesus had confronted Pilate, I wanted next to see the area where he grew up and began his ministry. My fellow passengers on the minibus were a fascinating lot. There were nine of us altogether, and, as we introduced ourselves to each other, it turned out that my companions were all Jewish tourists from various parts of the world, including England, the United States, Brazil, and South Africa. I was relieved to know there were no independent evangelists with the Last Days on their minds. We all had a jolly time, especially during an overnight visit at a kibbutz, where we ate a tasty fish dinner and played a rough game of touch football with some of the kibbutzniks. The following day, one of our first stops was at the spot on the Jordan River where—as the guides tell gullible tourists—Jesus was baptized by John the Baptist.

I had been forewarned, of course, that, while no one has the least idea of the actual location where this event took place, each guide nevertheless has a favorite riverside parking area where he or she can tell the story of Jesus' immersion by John and the riders can stretch their legs and gawk at the river. So I knew it was probably not the exact spot where the Gospels say the Spirit of God descended as a dove and blessed the work Jesus would soon begin. But I was taken in anyway. After all, it might be the spot. It did happen somewhere nearby. So I felt compelled to go beyond just the customary snapshot of the sluggish brown stream languidly flowing by. I wanted to wade in. As a thirteen-year-old boy, I had waded in once before. I had been baptized, following what our minister told us was the example of Jesus. He had referred to it then as "passing through Jordan." I simply could *not* look on motionless as the same water that Jesus was baptized in—albeit some nineteen hundred years later—splashed and gurgled by. So I took off my shoes and socks, rolled up my trousers, and strode in, first to my ankles, then to my knees, then up over the hems of my trousers to my thighs.

At first my fellow tourists smiled and made humorous comments. Then a kind of appalled silence fell over them. I had told two of them when the driver informed us we were going to stop at this baptismal location about my being baptized by immersion, and they probably wondered whether I was going to repeat the entire performance right before their eyes. I did not. After a few moments of standing in the Jordan, my toes caressing the sand and pebbles and the capillary action beginning to draw the dampness up toward my pockets, I turned and sloshed out. The other bus riders breathed a sigh of relief. They welcomed me ashore almost the way the aging deaconesses had helped me out of the baptismal pool at the little Baptist church in my hometown some forty-five years ago. As we climbed back in the bus and continued north, however, the subject of the conversation changed dramatically. We talked about Jesus.

It started when the English barrister asked me what it meant for me to "follow him." As I tried to answer, while putting my socks back on, everyone chimed in. Did I really believe he was God on earth? That he had walked on water and performed all those other miracles? Why had Christians for so many centuries blamed the Jews for what had happened to Jesus? As I rolled my slacks down and put my shoes back on, the conversation grew even more serious. Several of the passengers on the bus began to tell me what they thought about Jesus of Nazareth. Their comments were frank and wide-ranging. One man confessed there was no one in history he admired more. Another said Jesus' claim to be the messiah was either fraudulent or had been invented by the early Christians. A young woman from the United States told me she had cried after seeing a performance of *Jesus Christ Superstar* because at fifteen she had found him so attractive but that when she told her parents they had warned her that her crush was inappropriate, so she had switched to Paul Newman. The visitor from South Africa talked at length about his admiration for the Jewish painter Marc Chagall and described in enthusiastic detail how Chagall had tried to reappropriate the figure of Jesus into the long history of Jewish suffering and persecution by picturing a figure clothed in a prayer shawl and wearing phylacteries crucified amid pogroms and expulsions. A tourist from the United States, a cheerful elderly gentleman with very thick glasses, seemed pleased with himself when he remembered a phrase a rabbi had taught him many years ago, that "Jews can appreciate the faith *of* Jesus but not the faith *about* Jesus."

It went on and on. As the bus careened into the Galilean twilight, its penetrating horn rasping at cars that did not give way quickly enough, I marveled at the candor of the conversation. Here in the homeland of Jesus, perhaps as could happen nowhere else, Jews and Christians (at least one Christian) were talking about the man who has for centuries been both a bridge and a barrier between these two communities of faith, and for some reason it seemed more real than the discussions I had heard in advanced theology seminars.

Christians have had to struggle for many centuries with the fact that the founder of Christianity was Jewish and remained so throughout his entire life. They must constantly recognize that he had no Bible except what we call the Old Testament and that, if he were to return to planet earth today and seek a familiar house of worship in which to pray, he would no doubt seek out a synagogue, not a church. Jews, on the other hand, have had to watch as their holy books were incorporated, without their permission, into the Scriptures of another tradition and as one of their prophets was elevated to the kind of divine status that makes Jews uncomfortable. For centuries Jews were reluctant to think of Jesus as a prophet at all. Since the Holocaust and the birth of the state of Israel in 1948, however, the conversation between Jews and Christians has taken a wholly new turn: the figure of Jesus, rather than functioning as a taboo subject or an impossible obstacle, has begun to serve as one point of meeting. Just as they have in conversations with Hindus, Buddhists, and Muslims, Christians are discovering that, in the dialogue with Jews, the well-intentioned advice once given by so many cautious souls—that one should soft-pedal the person of Jesus in conversations with members of other faiths—is proving to be ill-founded.

Jesus' name is Yeshua, a late form of the Hebrew Yehoshuah, which means "Yahweh is salvation." The title "Messiah" or "Christ" that Christians attribute to Jesus was of course not originally part of his given name but a Christian confession of faith. Christians are left with the "stubborn, irreducible fact" that our faith is centered on a Jew. The shortest way to describe Christians is that we are those gentiles who try to serve and worship the God of the Jews. But the most uncomfortable fact for Christians to absorb is that, although we need Judaism, Judaism does not need Christianity. Christian theology is in large measure a series of interpretations of the events of Jewish history. But Jewish history ran its course for centuries before Christianity appeared, and it has no particular need to interpret the events of Christian history. The relationship between the two faiths is nonreciprocal. Still, a new phase in the long and troubled relationship between Jews and Christians now seems to have begun, and the importance of the state of Israel in the emergence of this new dialogue cannot be exaggerated.

Since 1948, for the first time since the Great Diaspora and since Constantine made Christianity the religion of the empire, Jews have had a homeland where they can express their views—even about the most sensitive subjects—without fear of repercussions from Christian prelates and princes. This was not the case during the centuries Jews lived under Christian rulers in what was often a hostile environment, when it would have been reckless indeed to talk about Jesus from a Jewish perspective. (It should be noted, of course, that many Jews lived in Muslim and other non-Christian countries, but they had less interest in the subject.) In the last forty years, however, since the founding of Israel, Jewish writing about Jesus, once a mere trickle, has become a torrent at both the scholarly and the lay level. After centuries of avoiding Jesus (with a few very notable exceptions), Jews now feel free to talk about him and, as my companions on the bus trip through Galilee so amply demonstrated, seem to want to.

Before such a dialogue can proceed, however, there is much bad history to be undone, or at least to be examined, carefully and pertinently on the part of Christians. We as Christians have perpetrated so much poor religious education that we have become the victims of our own ignorance. We need to know, for starters, that Jesus did not reject Judaism and that Christianity began as a tiny movement *within* Jesus' own ancestral faith. We need to be reminded that our church first came into being as a church of Jews, that it soon included both Jews and gentiles, and that only later did it go on to become a church mainly of gentiles.

We have also been misled by bad metaphors. Christianity has frequently been referred to as the "daughter" of Judaism. The problem with this analogy is that it conceals within itself the notion that the mother, having performed her birthing function, eventually grows old and dies while the daughter lives and grows into adulthood. Consequently, it reinforces the destructive idea that Christianity somehow "supersedes" Judaism and that therefore, as even the great Arnold Toynbee once wrote, the continued existence of Judaism after the coming of Christianity is something of an anomaly.

Recently, Alan Segal, in his excellent book *Rebecca's Children: Judaism and Christianity in the Roman World,* has suggested a much more fruitful metaphor. He demonstrates persuasively that the centuries immediately following the life of Jesus mark the beginning of not one but two great religious traditions in the West, Christianity and rabbinical Judaism. He sensibly argues that the proper figure of speech is, therefore, that of "Rebecca's children." Christianity and rabbinical Judaism spring from the same parent—ancient Judaism. They are more like Jacob and Esau who struggled with each other in the womb, who were born together, and who had to learn to live together as children of the same parent. Segal also shows that both rabbinical Judaism and Christianity took decisive steps toward a more universalistic understanding of the faith. Thus, the rabbinical movement, which traces its roots to before the destruction of the Temple in 70 C.E., imaginatively responded to that traumatic event by making Jewish faith more "portable." Because of the work of the rabbis, Judaism was no longer bound to a particular geographic location or to ritual sacrifice in the temple but could go anywhere, which it did. Christianity, on the other hand, also moved toward a more universal vision during the same period by abolishing the distinction between Jews and Gentiles and by claiming that, through Jesus as the Christ, the covenant had been enlarged to include those gentiles who chose to enter. Before the destruction of the Temple, Christianity had been no more than an apocalyptic sect within Judaism. Judaism had been something like a "civil religion" based in the Temple and in the land itself. From the ruins of the Temple there emerged, however, according to Segal, two sibling faiths forever linked by their common parent but with variant understandings of the nature of that universality.

I find Segal's metaphor particularly fruitful, although I realize it will not appeal to Christian fundamentalists—like my unsought acquaintance in Jerusalem—who insist that Jews must be converted to Jesus as the Christ if they are to be saved. I doubt it will appeal to those unlikely Jewish "fundamentalists" who are wondering how to rebuild the Temple and to reinstitute animal sacrifice. Ironically, these two factions have found some common ground. There are even indications that some American Christian fundamentalists have contributed financial and other support to the Jewish religious right in Israel. The Christians do so because in their scheme of things the rebuilding of the Temple will move us one step further along the path to the Last Days, the great battle of Armageddon, and the reappearance of the Messiah. Ironically, they also believe that, when the Messiah arrives to rescue the Jewish nation, the Jews will recognize that the Messiah is Christ and will be converted. The Jewish fundamentalists, of course, do not accept this final act in the apocalyptic script, but seem willing to receive support and encouragement for the initial phases. The two constitute an odd couple indeed, but their curious mutual parasitism suggests that the new dialogue between Christians and Jews can proceed at various levels, some of which are rather ominous.

The bad history we have learned, however, does not end with the formative period of Christian and Jewish rabbinical history. It goes on. Very early in the relationship between these two children of Rebecca, a serious feud began. Christian anti-Judaism appeared so quickly it has even found a place in the Christian Scriptures themselves. One has only to listen to the version of the Passion narrative in the Gospel of John, for example, to sense the anti-Judaistic polemical context in which it was written. Some of the characterizations of Judaism we find in the Gospel of Matthew are also inaccurate and invidious. There was, of course, an element of Jewish anti-Christianism as well. Jews were mainly concerned, however, not with gentile Christians, but with those Jews who believed that by becoming Christians they no longer had to observe the law. It was to apprehend these Jews—and not Christians as such—that Saul was making his trip to Damascus when he encountered his vision, changed his direction, and became the Apostle Paul.

When Christians came into imperial power, the situation became worse. Jews then had to live, not alongside another persecuted sect, but under Christian rulers who may or may not have been friendly to the Jewish community. During the first centuries of the Christian empire, Jews did not fare so badly. The Christian emperors closed pagan temples but not synagogues. As for the inner life of the Jewish community itself, this was one of its strongest and most energetic eras. The Jewish sages created the normative Judaism that gathered up all that had gone before and furnished the basis of all that was to follow.

Then, in the seventh century C.E., came Islam, which swept across Africa and up through the Iberian peninsula into southern France. It is a clear proof of how spiritually strong Judaism had become to point out that, although Christianity disappeared almost completely from many sections of the Muslim world, Judaism continued and in some places even thrived. In fact, Jews lived more freely and with less harassment under Islamic rule than they did under Christian princes. During the medieval period, the picture is not completely bleak. In some places, there was a good deal of collaboration and mutuality. For centuries, indeed, Christians, Jews, and Muslims lived on the Iberian peninsula cheek by jowl, sometimes in conflict, but often with a remarkable degree of mutual respect and reciprocity. Some scholars now believe that Saint John of the Cross may have picked up his most trenchant ideas from Muslim mystics.

The Crusades, however, poisoned the air in an ugly way. Frustrated Christian warriors often found that it was easier to march into a nearby Jewish village to rape and pillage than it was to make the arduous trip to the Palestine to cast out the infidels from the holy places. This domestic redirection of the Crusades was often fired by excited preachers who told the Crusaders that the Christ killers should not be allowed to escape the sword any more than the infidels should. Toward the waning of the Middle Ages, governments began expelling Jews from the countries of Western Europe. England expelled them in 1290 and France in 1394. In Russia and in Eastern Europe, Jews were restricted to particular areas and were frequently victimized by expulsions and pogroms. The Iberian peninsula, which has since acquired a bad reputation for religious intolerance, was an exception, at least for a time, to the general European anti-Judaism. Eventually, however, even those Jews were forced to convert or to leave, and Muslims were defeated by the force of arms. The last Islamic citadel, Granada, fell to Ferdinand and Isabella in 1492, the same year the Spanish Jews were expelled. Spain quickly became one of the least tolerant of the Christian kingdoms.

The baleful history of Christian contempt for Jews was unfortunately not corrected at the time of the Reformation. In *The Roots of Anti-Semitism in the Age of the Renaissance and Reformation,* Heiko Oberman documents the anti-Judaism of not just Luther, whose hateful attitude is widely known, but also of the allegedly more enlightened Erasmus. Luther lumped the Jews together with the Turks and the pope as the enemies of the gospel. In one of his more hysterical writings, entitled "Concerning the Jews," he goes so far as to suggest that, since Jews had become such a peril, their synagogues should be burned and their homes destroyed. He insists that Jews should be kept as captives in a stable and that their rabbis should be strictly forbidden to teach. It is chilling to recognize that, although Luther did not succeed in implementing his anti-Jewish program, almost everything he called for was eventually made official state policy by the German National Socialist regime in the 1930s and 1940s. Historians, of course, point out that the Nazis were also anti-Christian and that they advocated a reversion to Teutonic myths. But it is undeniable that they also drew on a long tradition of Christian anti-Semitism of which Luther's fulminations are only a small sample.

This historical Christian contribution to a process that terminated in Auschwitz makes me very reluctant to theologize about the Holocaust or to read Christian meanings into it. Almost everything any Christian has said on this subject sounds sour and wrong. As Emil Fackenheim has so poignantly reminded us, "A good Christian suggests that perhaps Auschwitz was a divine reminder of the suffering of Christ. Should he not ask instead whether his Master himself, had He been present at Auschwitz, would have resisted degradation and dehumanization? What are the sufferings of the Cross compared to those of a mother whose child is slaughtered to the sound of laughter or the strains of a Viennese waltz? The question may sound sacrilegious to Christian ears. Yet we dare not shirk it, for we—Christians as well as Jews—must ask: at Auschwitz, did the grave win the victory after all, or, worse than the grave, did the devil himself win?" When it comes to the Holocaust, perhaps the most appropriate Christian response is penitent silence and a firm resolution to prevent its recurrence.

But to dwell entirely on the bad history of the past is to do a disservice to the remarkable changes in Jewish-Christian relations that have occurred in recent years. As my lively bus ride to the Galilee showed me, the founding of the state of Israel produced an environment in which Jews could now feel free to deal with questions they had wisely avoided in more dangerous circumstances. But other things have happened too. In 1965, the Second Vatican Council officially removed negative mentions of Jews from the liturgy (although it is hard to foresee how such negative descriptions can be deleted from the scriptural texts themselves). In the scholarly world, there have been important developments as well. In Christian theology itself, tracing the origins of Christianity not just to the Old Testament but to first-century Judaism has become a larger subject of study, especially since the uncovering of the Dead Sea Scrolls. There is also a vastly increased interest among Christians in the tradition of rabbinical Judaism from the biblical period to the present. It must also be said, however, that the growing attention focused on this tradition has resulted largely from the efforts of (mainly Jewish) scholars of Judaism who have introduced the study of Judaica into universities and colleges all over the Western world.

One can reasonably hope that much of the ignorance that has kept Christians and Jews apart and perpetuated misunderstanding is beginning to decline. At the divinity school where I am a professor, for example, we have recently instituted a permanent and fully tenured professorship in Jewish religious thought—the Albert A. List Chair in Jewish Studies. The establishment of this chair clearly indicates that our faculty considers Judaism to be not a kind of leftover anomaly but a permanent and vigorous partner in a pluralistic religious world.

A parallel development has appeared among Jewish scholars as well. Jews are showing increased interest both in the New Testament period and in Jesus. Much of this interest springs from what Rabbi Alan Mittleman calls the Jews' "creative obsession with the richness of their own history." He puts it this way.

> In the writing of Jewish theologians, historians, Bible scholars and literary men and women, Jesus has been—tentatively at least—returning to his ancestral home. For 200 years, beginning with Moses Mendelssohn and his contemporaries, Jewish authors have been overturning the medieval Jewish caricature of Jesus and discovering in him a like-minded Jew. While not symmetrical with the Christian theological reappraisal of Judaism, there is a certain similarity. It is, simply, that the Jewish rediscovery of Jesus—like the Christian reappraisal of Judaism—is rooted in a new appreciation of Jewish history. . . . The "homecoming of Jesus," therefore, is an aspect of the modern Jew's act of historically oriented self-discovery, or of self-recovery. It is an aspect of the modern Jew's search for essence and definition.

My conversation with my fellow tourists in the little speeding bus echoed the "homecoming of Jesus" Rabbi Mittleman refers to, but it also reminded me that the recent reemergence of Jewish interest in Jesus builds on a scholarly tradition that has been there for a long time.

The question about Jesus Jewish thinkers have pondered can be put very simply. Can Jesus have either a moral or even a religious significance for Jews? It has long been recognized that, for Jews, the prophet from Nazareth can have a *cultural* meaning, but the question I have mentioned places the issue of Jesus' significance for Jews at a much deeper level. It is an old discussion. Max Nordau, a collaborator with Theodore Herzl in founding the modern Zionist movement, wrote at the beginning of the century, "Jesus is the soul of our soul as he is the flesh of our flesh. Who then would want to exclude him from the Jewish people?" The question, however, is not the exclusion of Jesus from the Jewish people. It is whether as a part of that people Jesus can be seen to have a positive rather than a negative religious significance. Schalom ben-Chorin answers the question as follows: "Jesus is a central figure in history and in the history of Jewish faith. He is a part not only of our past and present but also of our future, no less than are the prophets of the Hebrew Bible, whom we can also see not just in the light of the past."

The reader of this telling sentence is intrigued but also left to wonder just what part Jesus is to play. Ben-Chorin opens the door for conversation but also sets one of the limits of the Jewish appreciation for the religious significance of Jesus: "I feel," he says, "his brotherly hand which grasps mine so I can follow him . . . but it is *not* the hand of the Messiah. This hand marked with scars. It is not a *divine* but a *human* hand in the lines of which is engraved the most profound suffering." Then ben-Chorin goes on to make the statement that perhaps my fellow tourist's rabbi had once read and pours a lot into a few words. "The faith *of* Jesus," he writes, underlining "of," "unites us but faith *in* Jesus divides us."

In the conversation on the bus, I pointed out to the smiling gentleman with the thick glasses that some present-day

Christian theologians, especially in Latin America, believe precisely that it is the faith *of* Jesus that is central. Jon Sobrino, for example, in his *Christology at the Crossroads,* argues that neither Jesus nor God but Jesus' own faith in the coming of the Reign of God should be the focus of Christian faith. We have faith *in* Jesus because he is the enactor and announcer of the coming of the Reign of God.

On the question of the significance of Jesus for his own people, it seems inappropriate for an outsider to say very much. It is a topic that Jews themselves must be left to deal with if and when they choose to. However, as one of those "outsiders" to whom Jesus also addressed his message, I have never found anyone who has written with quite the eloquence of Martin Buber. Buber, considering what the man from Nazareth might mean to his own kinsmen, affirms the spiritual significance of Jesus while at the same time insisting that Jews will always have their own way of understanding what this significance is. In a famous letter to Franz Werfel that he wrote in 1917, Buber responded to Werfel's inquiry about his view of Jesus by emphasizing the centrality of the human response to God rather than God's initiative. The letter is worth quoting at length:

> It is not I who wait for God, but God who waits for me. God waits so that He can say to you, to me, to every single person what according to the report in the Hebrew Gospel the Spirit said to Jesus when he raised him in baptism to sonship: My son I have awaited you in all the prophets, that you should come and that I should find peace in you. You are indeed my peace.
>
> No, dear friend, nothing is imposed on us by God, everything is expected. And you rightly say, it is up to us whether we want to live the true life in order to perfect it in our uniqueness. But according to the Christian teaching which has perverted the meaning and ground of Jesus,

> it is not up to us but depends on whether we are chosen. But our teaching is: what counts is not whether God has chosen me but that I choose God. For it is really not God's affair to choose or reject. In so far as it refers the person to grace, that teaching, which calls itself Christian, hinds him from decision, the *metanoia* proclaimed by Jesus . . . therefore I shall fight for Jesus and against Christianity.

A few lines later, Buber continues with a description of the Reign of God that is similar to the one we find in liberation theology:

> What Jesus calls the Kingdom—no matter how tinged with a sense of the world's end and of miraculous transformation it may be—is no other-world consolation, no vague heavenly bliss. Nor is it an ecclesiastical or cultic association, a church. It is the perfect life of man with man, true community, and as such God's immediate realm, God's basilea, God's earthly kingdom.

This remarkable reaching out by Jews toward the man whose name has for so many years been used as the pretense for their oppression obviously involves some enormous dangers. Christians must exercise great caution in responding to it. As Karl Plank has written (in *Night and White Crucifixion*) of the art of Marc Chagall, "To depict the Jew on the cross after the war was to confront a stronger taboo, for to do so required the victim to draw from the oppressor's cultural tradition. And the potential for being misunderstood would be enormous: by fellow victims who would perceive apostasy and betrayal instead of solidarity, by oppressors who would hear forgiving consolation instead of indictment." The new Jewish interest requires at least as energetic an effort on the part of Christians to redefine our understanding of Jews in such a way that they are no longer made the objects of the teaching of contempt or seen as historical curios from a previous period in history.

It has been rightly suggested that one route to this redefinition must begin with Saint Paul's passage in the eleventh chapter of Romans about the relations between Christians and Jews. A careful reading of that famous text makes it clear that, for Paul, the Covenant God made with Israel continues in force just as it did with Noah, Abraham, and Moses. Paul speaks plainly. He compares the gentiles to a "wild olive shoot which is grafted onto the tree, the olive tree of Israel." He goes on to point out that we who are so grafted should not boast since God is fully capable of choosing other shoots. Paul insists the gifts and the call of God are entirely irrevocable. The gospel of Jesus does not supersede God's call to the people of Israel or negate the Covenant made with them. It has the purpose of calling the gentiles so that they too may share in God's blessings.

A careful study of this central passage can teach us a number of things about the dialogue between Jews and Christians. First, the God about whom Paul is speaking is not some general God of the religious consciousness or of a vague monotheism. This God is the God of Abraham and Sarah, the God of the Covenant. Therefore, for Paul the question is *not* one of the relation between Jews and Christians at all. Rather, it is that of the relation between Israel (for the Jews continue to be God's people), on the one hand, and "the nations," on the other hand. Paul does not even use the word "Christian" in this discussion, although he undoubtedly knew the term, which was already in circulation at the time. It helps us today to understand the so-called Christian-Jewish dialogue to see that, for Paul, it had nothing to do with a conversation between two religious traditions but with the question of how all the other peoples of the globe were to enter the one Covenant of the one God.

Paul's experience on the road to Damascus was not a "conversion," and must not be understood as his "becoming a Christian." Paul did not become a member of another religious community. Rather, what came to him in that blinding light was a new conviction about the way he should fulfill his vocation as a Hebrew. He was not converted but "called" to a prophetic vocation both to his own people and to the gentiles. His vocation, he believed, was to proclaim the good news of the enlargement of the Covenant both to those who were already inside (the Jews) and to those who had previously been outside (the rest of us). Paul's view of Gentiles and Jews appears most graphically in the second chapter of the Epistle to the Ephesians, which, although some scholars believe it was not written by Paul himself, certainly expresses his persepctive on this issue. The text reads, "Remember that at one time you Gentiles in the flesh were . . . separated from Christ, alienated from the commonwealth of Israel, and strangers to the covenants of promise having no hope and without God in the world." "But now," the writer continues, "in Christ Jesus you who once were far off have been brought near."

For Paul, who calls himself a "Hebrew of the Hebrews," Jesus signifies that the God who created the world, who called Sarah and Abraham, who gave humankind the law at Sinai, and who spoke through the prophets had now taken another decisive step. This time, the same God was inviting the Gentiles into the Covenant, thus reconciling alienated peoples to each other. Again, it is important to emphasize that the peoples who are reconciled are not Christians and Jews but Israel and the nations.

In the light of this historic text about dialogue, Paul's often misunderstood criticisms of the Jews in the Epistle to the Romans must be read with great care. They are not the reproofs of an outsider who has now left his religious community to become the member of another one. They are rather the words of an insider who—like the earlier prophets—chides his fellow Jews *because* he is an insider. Paul speaks here like Isaiah and Amos and Jeremiah. He continues the tradition of the prophets who lovingly taught their own people. This is quite different from sniping at them from a position outside that community of faith.

As we neared the hotel where we were to spend our evening together, my fellow passengers on the little bus began to ask each other some very practical questions. What would it mean, they fantasized, if Christians and Jews could put away the suspicion and animosity that has distorted our relations over the centuries? The tourist from South Africa, who was very sympathetic to the efforts of the black freedom struggle, put it as well as anyone. If in fact, he said, both Jews and Christians are trying to do the will of the same God, then we should be trying to increase the realm of freedom—because God has always favored the poor and insisted that how we treat the stranger in our midst is the real test. I told him I saw nothing to disagree with in this statement. But no sooner had those words left my lips than the bus suddenly slowed to a crawl and—as if to underline what my friend had just said about the strangers in our midst—we found ourselves grinding slowly through a gang of workers who were repairing the road. Suddenly all the conversations stopped. Everyone looked out at this crowd of laughing, perspiring men, whom we all knew were Palestinians. They stopped and stared back. No one—inside or outside—waved or smiled. For two, maybe three minutes, the bus inched along. Then it stopped while one of the workers directed two cars coming from the opposite direction to drive through. The silence in the bus continued. After a moment the man signaled to our driver, who steered us slowly back onto the hard surface, slipped into second and then high gear, and took off for our evening's destination.

We had never been in danger. But even after the bus was clipping along at fifty miles an hour again, for some reason no one talked. Why, I wondered. Was it embarrassment? Awkwardness? Or was it perhaps that we all shared an unspoken recognition that the question of who is the stranger in whose land is not at all clear when one is driving through what some Israelis call the "occupied territories" and others refer to as "Greater Israel"? Nothing is ever simple in the Middle East, but, as the decades-long Israeli-Palestinian struggle has worsened in recent years, what was already complex has now become downright convoluted. Do Christians have any right whatever, or any obligation, to play a role?

Johann Baptist Metz, the German Catholic theologian, once wrote an eloquent essay about the complicity of Christians in the Jewish Holocaust. In the course of that article he said, "We Christians can never go back behind Auschwitz: to go beyond Auschwitz, if we see clearly, is impossible for us by ourselves. It is possible only together with the victims of Auschwitz." This strikes me as a wise and helpful comment. But like many such comments it raises almost as many questions as it answers. What does it mean for Christians and Jews to journey together when the strife within Israel threatens not only the lives of those immediately involved in it but has become the tinderbox of a conflagration that could escalate into a much wider war?

One current Jewish writer, Marc Ellis, has responded to Metz by paraphrasing him in these words: "We Jews can never go back behind empowerment: to go beyond empowerment, if we see clearly, is impossible for us by ourselves. It is possible only with the victims of our empowerment." This is also an astute observation, but it still does not answer the question of *what* Christians can or should do in light of the deteriorating situation in Israel.

When the conversation on the minibus finally started again it was subdued and sporadic. And it was about something else: cameras and film and how good it would feel to get to the inn. It was not about Palestinians or Israelis or Jews or Christians or Jesus. I sat quietly and gazed out the window at the twilight. It was not going to be easy, I realized, this journey of dialogue some Christians and some Jews have embarked on together. The fact that among the Christians most needed in the dialogue are the Palestinian ones makes it even harder but even more urgent. The pain and anger and guilt that lurk along the way will tempt us at every step to allow the dialogue to deteriorate into something nicely "religious," a theological or historical conversation that steers away from potentially divisive issues. It could become a dialogue of the devout, so rarefied it doesn't ruffle anyone. It could melt away into yet another version of that endless "spiritual quest" that lures so many seekers so far into the elysium they forget the nettlesome issues people of faith have to wrestle with on *terra firma*. Yet it seemed clearer than ever to me during that instructive bus ride that a genuine Jewish-Christian dialogue cannot take place in a sealed vehicle while the others stare in the windows. It must be pursued in the ordinary rough-and-tumble world of suffering, hope, disappointment, and perseverance, not as the attempt to achieve unforgettable peak experiences or mystical rapture. Indeed, although Christians can drift easily into this kind of ecstatic euphoria, it is precisely our bond with the Jewish people that constantly brings us back to where God really is in the world, and that keeps us from soaring too high into the zenith.

Christians certainly need Jews. Without them in our past, we would have had no Bible, no Jesus, no knowledge of God. Without them in our present, we cannot understand God, the world, or ourselves. But we Christians must also recognize that although Jews are central to our faith, we are not central to theirs. As Christians we *must* talk about Jesus, and, as my fellow passengers on the tourist bus taught me, Jews are willing to talk about him too. But what divides Christians from Jews is not that we have different views of Jesus (which of course we do). What divides us is that Jews have something we do not. They have Torah. They have God's gift of both a written revelation in Scripture (which we can share up to a point) and an equally authoritative oral tradition codified by the rabbis into the Mishnah and the Talmud, which we do not have and never can. When the Temple was razed in 70 C.E., Christians came to believe that Jesus the Christ had taken its place. Jews believed its place was assumed by Torah, a living and breathing ongoing revelation. Jacob Neusner puts it this way:

> The symbol of Torah is multidimensional. It includes the striking detail that whatever the most recent rabbi is destined to discover through proper exegesis of the tradition is as much a part of the Torah revealed to Moses as is a sentence of Scripture itself. It is therefore possible to participate even in the giving of the law by appropriate, logical inquiry into the law. God himself, studying and living by Torah, is believed to subject himself to the same rules of logical inquiry. When an earthly court overruled the testimony, delivered through miracles, of the heavenly one, God rejoiced, crying out, "My sons have conquered me!"—so the sages believed. In a word, before us is a mythicoreligious system in which earth and heaven correspond to one another, with Torah—in place of Temple—the model of both.

A fundamental ground rule for any dialogue between Christians and Jews must be this: there can never be a question of Christians attempting to convert Jews to Christianity. The whole idea is a contradiction in terms. It is those of us who are called Christians who are, we believe, "adopted" into the Covenant God made with the Jews, not the other way around. We are the latecomers, the wild twig that is grafted onto the existing tree. When I told one of my fellow bus passengers that the New Testament scholar Krister Stendahl once called Christians "honorary Jews," he laughed. He said that he was fond of collecting the religious sentiments expressed on bumper stickers and that one he frequently sees is "I found it" (usually with an exclamation mark) on the bumper sticker of enthusiastic Christians. He said that a Unitarian neighbor of his sports a sticker that adamantly insists, "I am still looking." Then he added that he had once thought of pasting a sticker on his own bumper that would read "We never lost it."

I told him his theology deserved an A+. It is we Gentile Christians who, according to the Apostle Paul, were once the lost and wandering ones "outside the Covenant of Israel." It is we who have been "converted" and have entered as newcomers. I also reminded my friend that, although the other bumper stickers he mentioned started with "I," it was significant that his began with "we." This says something important to us about the faith of Israel: it is not the faith of individuals but the faith of a people.

Christians are slowly learning to welcome "otherness," religious, cultural, and otherwise, not as an inconvenience we must somehow put up with but as a gift of God, a reminder of our human finitude and of the unsearchable richness of the Holy One. However, it seems increasingly clear to me that, as urgent as conversations with Buddhists or Hindus may be, we must come to terms first with those "others" who have lived in our very midst from the beginning. Dialogue is important wherever it occurs, but at times it seems that working so hard on conversations with other religious traditions while ignoring the otherness that is closest to us can be a kind of escape. Those who remain God's original chosen people continue to live as our neighbors and friends and even as our husbands and wives. In the past, Christians have dealt with this closeness in all the worst ways. Perhaps God is giving us another chance.

We can neither deny nor minimize the differences between Christians and Jews. Jews do not accept the pivotal Christian claim that in Jesus the Covenant people has been enlarged to include Christians. This difference is not trivial and should not be overlooked. Nonetheless, recalcitrantly, stubbornly, and slowly, we Christians are coming to recognize that our former ways of relating to Jews—conversion, expulsion, destruction—were always terribly wrong. Can we believe that now, after nearly two millennia of doing it badly, Christians are learning that the two children of Rebecca can live as siblings?

When I think of this question, I am enormously encouraged by the statement on Judaism recently adopted by the United Church of Christ. It is an eloquent affirmation of the continuing validity of God's Covenant with the Jewish people and a reminder of the deeds for which we as Christians hope to be forgiven. The text runs as follows:

> We in the United Church of Christ acknowledge that the Christian Church has, throughout much of its history, denied God's continuing convenantal relationship with the Jewish people expressed in the faith of Judaism. This denial has often led to outright rejection of the Jewish people and to theologically and humanly intolerable violence.

> Faced with this history from which we as Christians cannot, and must not, disassociate ourselves, we ask for God's forgiveness through our Lord Jesus Christ. We pray for divine grace that will enable us, more firmly than ever before, to turn from this path of rejection and persecution to affirm that Judaism has not been superseded by Christianity; that Christianity is not to be understood as the successor religion to Judaism; God's covenant with the Jewish people has not been abrogated. God has not rejected the Jewish people; God is faithful in keeping covenant.

This says a lot. But it says it in words. And Jews have heard eloquent words on the subject before.

When our bus reached the hotel, most of the passengers raced for the showers, but Alex, the English lawyer, and I went into the bar for a cool drink. Apparently with the others out of earshot, he now felt free to voice some misgivings. It was certainly fine that I felt the way I did, he said, but was there any real hope that most Christians would begin to change their attitude toward Jews? Or was this dialogue business really just one more new strategy in the old game, a slicker soft-sell gimmick to nudge Jews closer to the baptismal font?

At first, I was a little hurt by his remark. But then I thought about my eschatology teacher in the sunglasses, with his crazed vision of cosmic battles and the mass conversion of Jews, and I shook my head. My fellow tourist waited, but I knew I had little basis on which to reassure him. It has been a long, sad story. One of the first documents Christian theology students study comes from the second century C.E. It is by Justin Martyr and is called *Dialogue with the Jew Trypho*. But it is not a dialogue. It is a trick polemic in which the Christian Justin tries to prove Trypho wrong and to demonstrate that Christ had superseded Judaism. That pseudodialogue, which began so early, has lasted too long. Alex knew, and I know, that, since this phoniness has been perpetrated mainly by Christians, Christians will have to do most of the work in restoring credibility to what is beyond any doubt the most important dialogue of all.

6

The Search for a Soviet Christ

In the Soviet writer Chingiz Aitmatov's novel *The Executioner's Block,* first published in 1985, a pious Russian Orthodox seminarian named Abdias Kallistratov, the son of a priest, is expelled from the theological school because he asks too many questions. Deprived of his original vocation, Kallistratov begins to work for a Komosomol newspaper. After a series of adventures, he is eventually arrested—having refused to join a campaign to exterminate excess antelopes—and tried in Stalinist style as an "enemy of the state." At the age of thirty-three, he is finally put to death. Through it all Kallistratov retains a kind of moral simplicity and purity. He never loses what the author calls "his interior flame."

Aitmatov's book has caused something of a sensation in the Soviet Union, and the debate it has touched off is testing the limits of *glasnost'*. Some critics have compared Abdias to Prince Myshkin in Dostoyevski's *The Idiot,* a traditional Russian Christ figure but this time one of Soviet vintage, mercilessly squeezed between a rigid church and an atheistic state, institutions Aitmatov characterizes as twin "mastodons."

Others call the book jumbled and derivative. Hard-liners see it as proof positive that the current generation of writers has gone soft on religion. But no one denies the urgency of its underlying question. Is the whole idea of a "Soviet Christ" an oxymoron? Or is a new representation of Jesus emerging, as it has elsewhere, one that combines the classic features of the Russian Christ of Orthodox icons and Dostoyevsky with the experience of seventy years of Soviet history?

During the early summer of 1987, I found myself living in Moscow with time on my hands and Aitmatov's question on my mind. I had accompanied my wife, a historian of Russia, who was there as an exchange scholar. But since I had little to do myself, I occupied my time by visiting historical sites, practicing Russian, walking through the streets and markets, and exploring the endless reaches of the subway system. In the course of my wanderings, I decided one day to stroll through the inner court of the Kremlin grounds—which are open to the public—to visit the splendid churches there, now museums, which date far back into the imperial period. Taking the subway to Red Square, I got off, walked through the outer gate, and spent several hours in the Uspenski (Assumption) Cathedral, the Blagoveschenski (Annunciation) Cathedral, and the Cathedral of the Archangel. I was stunned, overwhelmed by the sense of an interrupted but still living history and by the brooding dignity of the icons, especially the severe renditions of Christ. I was glad I had not come with a tour. Alone, I could stand in front of any icon for as long as I needed to, let my eyes accustom themselves to the darkness, and allow the quiet power of the Russian Christ—the one Russian believers say continues to suffer through all history and for all humanity—to sink in. I did not have to listen to the chatter of the Intourist guides or rush on to the next stop.

After a couple of hours, I returned to the bright sunlight of the courtyard. As I did, a young Russian man, who appeared to be about thirty, introduced himself to me in excellent English. He told me he had noticed I was a foreigner, probably an American, and that instead of rushing past the "holy icons," as he called them, I seemed to be absorbed in them. Was I by any chance a believer?

At first I did not know quite how to respond. Was this the beginning of a KGB entrapment? Did he want to buy my running shoes? I hesitated. But something in his straightforward manner and earnest smile put me at ease. I told him I was in fact a believer and that I had sensed something compelling about the icons. We started to stroll as we talked, first past the statue of Lenin, then out the gate and into Red Square. Still talking, we walked over to the Arbat, the picturesque old quarter of Moscow. As we walked, he introduced himself. He was a television writer and had come to the Kremlin in connection with a show they were preparing. With an hour free until his next appointment, he had wandered into the Uspenski and noticed me. After we chatted a while, I ventured my question. I asked him what he knew about the widely reported "return to religion" among Russian intellectuals. Was it really going on? Was it widespread? What did it mean?

He stopped walking to answer. "I suspect," he said, "that I would have to be counted among them." I told him I was very interested, not just objectively but personally, and that I wanted to speak with those for whom the quest for a new spirituality had become in some way their own. Could he help? My new acquaintance, whom I'll call "Yuri," told me he had to get back to work then (he was already an hour late, he said) but made a date to meet me at the Nova Devichy monastery for Vespers the following day, Sunday. At that time, he said, he would introduce me to a friend of his who was exactly the right person to help me. We exchanged phone numbers, shook hands, and parted just in front of the multihued Saint Basil's Cathedral in Red Square.

For the rest of Saturday and most of Sunday, I wondered whether I would ever see Yuri again and whether anyone would be willing to talk seriously with me about the questions I had on my mind. I doubted anyone would, and I decided that, while I would go to the Vespers at the Nova Devichy, I would hold out no real hope of seeing Yuri.

But, when I climbed out of my taxi, he was there, standing with his friend, a slightly younger man, just outside the gate to the monastery. He introduced me to Karol, and, right away, whatever doubts I had harbored about whether people would want to talk with me about this topic began to melt. I spent my remaining weeks in Moscow doing little else.

For many Russian intellectuals today, talking has become more than the pleasure it has always been (remember those endless discussions that run through pages and pages of the great Russian novels?). Since *glasnost'*, it has taken on the quality of a sacred duty. As one writer told me later, "Every day we have to widen the perimeter a little and create more cleared space so that the cautious souls will feel free to come out of their holes." Since religious questions are flying again and talking with foreigners—once a forbidden pastime—is one benefit of *glasnost'*, I had no problem finding conversation partners.

I stayed clear of both official interpreters and official church leaders. I wanted neither the government nor the ecclesial line. Though my Russian is weak, the mainly well educated people I talked with either knew some English or had a friend who could translate. By the time I came home, I had met poets, editors, translators, screenwriters, and musicians—enough different people to persuade me that the search for a Soviet Christ is neither ephemeral nor faddish. It is real, though amorphous, sometimes tentative, and still very fragile. It also means different things to different people. Perhaps the best way to convey a feeling for it all is to introduce some of the seekers and believers I talked with. I have changed their names, not to protect them from official harassment, which none of them thought likely, but to respect the privacy of people who were willing to speak quite openly about what is after all a very personal matter.

I started with Ivan, whom I met through Yuri's friends. Along with Ivan's wife, teenage son, and eight-year-old daughter, we met in Ivan's apartment, where he invited me to share a late supper. The apartment was an ample one, though not commodious, located in one of those endless strings of high-rise apartment houses surrounded by parks and greenbelts on the suburban fringe of Moscow. The walls of every room were lined with notes, mementos, postcards, and books in several languages, but with Russian titles predominating. Ivan is a professional translator of poetry from modern European languages into Russian. A square, handsome man in his middle forties with a sprinkling of grey hair around the temples, he has an intense expression in his eyes but a warm and ready smile. He told me he had been raised in a completely nonreligious family with a Jewish ethnic background. His parents had been neither friendly nor unfriendly toward religion. They were simply interested in other things. When he became personally concerned about a religious quest, he found himself attracted to Russian Orthodoxy in part because there seemed to be little else available and also because it suited his aesthetic temperament.

Why had Ivan not sought out the Soviet Jewish community when he began his adult quest? When I asked him that, he seemed saddened by the question. He answered by telling me what I had also heard from other sources, namely, that, although the Jewish minority in Russia remains a cultural and intellectual force far beyond its size, years of discrimination—and the emigration that hardship has caused—have weakened its religious vitality. Here and there one sees signs that the phenomenal liveliness that once characterized this beleaguered segment of world Jewry might be returning. But the signs are few and the obstacles many. In any case, for Ivan, where a spiritual quest seemed to have been fused with a search for a cultural heritage, it did not appear to be a viable option.

He had also, he told me, always loved the icons, even as a boy. You could see that he still did. There were icons on the walls of every room in the apartment, with a special cluster in the corner of the main living room, where, as is often the case in Moscow apartments, we gathered around the table for supper. Before we ate, Ivan invited me to join the entire family in standing to face the icons while they repeated the Lord's Prayer in Russian, crossing themselves in the Orthodox right-to-left style as they said "Amen." After the meal of soup, ground meat cakes, fresh radishes, and savory black bread with butter and sour cream (there was no alcohol), Ivan and I talked about his pilgrimage.

I asked him first to tell me about the icons in the corner. We walked over to them, and he pointed out a Theotokos, the mother of God in one of her most popular Russian apparitions as our Lady of Vladimir. Another was Jesus Christ as Pantocrator, the hollow-eyed, suffering ruler of the cosmos. There were also Saint Michael the Archangel and two unfamiliar Russian saints who turned out to be an obscure bishop and a metropolitan from earlier centuries. While Ivan still loved the icons, as our conversation unfolded it became clear to me that his faith was part and parcel with a wider affection for "tradition," which he believes is an indispensable component in a truly human life. For example, when we talked about the religious denominations in the West, of which he was somewhat familiar, he asked me with a puzzled look if there was really a debate going on about the ordination of women to the priesthood. When I told him that there was and that some churches had in fact already ordained women, he shook his head. He did not, he said, agree with such "departures." He described himself as a man who at a certain stage in his life enjoyed and even embraced novelty—the latest styles in art, music, and literature. Since embracing Orthodoxy, however, he said he had become more conservative in nearly all his views and that his suspicion of modernity extended to the works of the most prominent contemporary Soviet poets, among them Yevtushenko and Vosnezensky. He thinks they are too interested in effect and success, too willing to compromise the moral vocation of the poet in order to achieve recognition and privilege. On the other hand, he continues to love and cherish the heroine of recent Russian poetry, Nachmatova, who suffered such persecution during the Stalin years. Two prominent pictures of Nachmatova, one in each of the major rooms of the house, testified to Ivan's devotion. Although her photographs were hung several feet from the icons, I had the feeling that, in Ivan's pantheon, she was a kind of Theotokos of the poetic vocation.

After we'd been talking for a few minutes, I began to sense a certain awkwardness in Ivan. Perhaps he recognized how often a traditional Orthodox believer can sound intransigent and even condescending to religious believers from other traditions. There was an uneasy pause. Then somehow the conversation turned to American jazz, and Ivan brightened. Leaning back in his chair, he plunged into an animated discussion of his early love affair with Duke Ellington and Charlie Parker and of his continuing enjoyment of American big band music. He described how as a young man during the war he eagerly tuned in the old Armed Forces radio station and how he still listens to jazz on the Voice of America. He told me that he had understood completely when some years earlier a prominent Russian poet, on returning from America, had told him that the most memorable moment of his visit had been meeting Gerry Mulligan in a New York nightclub. It occurred to me as he spoke that this was at least one feature of his earlier life that had not been greatly altered by his religious conversion. I doubted, however, that he would think well of any of the recent jazz liturgies or that he knew that his revered Ellington himself had composed one shortly before he died. I decided not to say anything about them.

After the discussion about jazz had run its course, I asked Ivan whether, in his view, the "return" of Soviet intellectuals to religion was real. He told me that, although part of it certainly bore the marks of a fad, there was also something deeper and longer lasting going on. He added, however, in slightly regretful tones, that he was not at all sure the Russian Orthodox church was in any position to respond to this interest. I listened carefully. It was the first time he had voiced even a hint of criticism about his church. A few weeks ago, he told me, he had asked his own priest why there seemed to be no teaching in their church. Why, he wondered, was there not something to supplement the liturgy and the music that would inform people about the history and theology of Orthodoxy? "What the priest told me," he said "was, 'The icons teach us all we need to know.'" He punctuated the sentence with his hands thrown up in a gesture that could have meant either that he wished the priest had said more or that the statement revealed something of the mystery and genius of Orthodoxy.

When we talked about his work as a translator and about literature in general, Ivan told me that for his own personal reading he has returned to the classics, especially Dostoyevski, Tolstoy, and Cervantes, that he does not enjoy contemporary literature nearly as much as he once did. "Take Kafka," he said. "I once *loved* to read Kafka, but now I feel . . ." Here, he paused and shrugged. He did not want to seem down on all recent literature and hastened to tell me that among American writers the one he appreciated most was Saul Bellow. He thought that *Mr. Sammler's Planet* was the best recent American novel. It was hard not to like a man who could appreciate both Saul Bellow and Charlie Parker. I sensed that Ivan was someone for whom Orthodoxy provided a personal grounding and a worldview, that he lived it without lopping off his own tastes and idiosyncrasies. It helped him sort out and make judgments, but for him it was anything but a closed system. Still, I could not help pondering his remark about the lack of teaching in the Orthodox church. He was a man who loved ideas as well as icons. He seemed to combine not quite successfully the old-style Slavophile's suspicion of Western overintellectualizing with a desire to explore the theological concepts of his newly discovered tradition in a rigorous way. As Ivan walked me to the taxi stand and embraced me when the cab pulled up, I knew that I had been speaking with a pilgrim who was still on the way.

The day after my conversation with Ivan, I met "Elena," an acquaintance he had called on my behalf, at a restaurant in downtown Moscow. She had invited me for a late lunch. A tall woman in her early fifties, she wore a tailored suit and a white blouse and had gathered her graying auburn hair in a ponytail. Seated at a comfortable table in the wood-beamed dining room, Elena thoughtfully ordered what turned out to be the best meal I ate in Moscow—borscht, salad, pork chops with broccoli and potatoes, a fine rosé wine, and coffee.

The conversation was anything but trivial. Elena wanted to talk about the philosophical and moral question of "betrayal." She told me that she, and many other writers who had lived through the Stalin years, had become painfully aware that tyranny is possible only if people are willing to inform on each other, sometimes in large ways, but often in small ones. Repression relies on such informers. She told me that she could not stop thinking about betrayal, not the kind, she said, that occurs under torture or threat, but the kind one finds oneself slipping into, even after vowing never to let it happen. This was the reason, she said, that she was drawn time and again to the story of Peter's denial of Christ, about which she had recently written a short play. She puffed on her cigarette and smiled: the director told her, she said, "that he was aware of the need to use the new liberty of *glasnost'* but was not sure that the Moscow theater public was ready for a play drawn directly from the Bible." She still had not decided whether to rewrite the play, to press for its production, or to wait until the atmosphere seemed more conducive to it.

By the time I spoke with Elena, I had discovered that Aitmatov's novel and his question about the possibility of a Soviet Christ functioned as something of an ink blot test in my conversations with Moscow intellectuals. Everyone had read it, and everyone had a strong opinion about it. It seemed to allow them to speak about themselves and issues of faith in a more relaxed way since they did not have to focus on their own personal quest so directly. When I brought this issue up with Elena, she drew a long inhalation on her Marlboro, took a sip of rosé, leaned back, and frowned ever so slightly. When she began to speak, I could tell by her tone that she was not favorably disposed toward *The Executioner's Block* but that she wanted to phrase her criticism in a measured way. The trouble with Aitmatov, she finally said, was that he wrote as though he had just discovered the Bible last week and was suddenly inspired to use it for his novel. One could stretch a point, she explained, and read his narrative as an example of self-conscious simplicity, but, on the other hand, it might also be just plain primitive. Her smile left little doubt about which interpretation she herself favored.

The novel itself weaves an intricate web of three stories. The first story concerns a Kirghiz shepherd who bears the odd name of "Boston" Ourkountchiev, a nonconformist who constantly attracts attention and difficulty to himself simply because he criticizes the stupid directives handed down by party and bureaucratic elites. The second concerns the wolves of the steppes, whom Aitmatov depicts as victims of the human predators despoiling the wilds. The third is the story of the seminarian Kallistratov. After his expulsion from seminary, Kallistratov infiltrates a band of drug dealers in order to obtain a story for the Komsomol newspaper he is working for and accompanies them when they make a trip to harvest marijuana deep inside one of the Asian republics. When he decides he cannot go through with it and tries to persuade the dealers to give up their trade, they beat him up and throw him out of a moving train. Miraculously, he survives, and then writes his article for the paper. The editors refuse to print it, however, telling him it would be damaging to the reputation of the country, and they fire him. Penniless, he hooks up with a gang that guns down antelopes for their fur. Once again unable to carry through his assignment, he is judged and condemned by the mob (whose leader is clearly modeled on Stalin). The theological dimensions of the book become most explicit in the long dialogues between Kallistratov and his two principal antagonists, the father superior at the seminary and the chief of the drug traffickers, who bear an ominous similarity to each other. They both expatiate at length about God and the meaning of power.

The Executioner's Block contains a long flashback to Pontius Pilate's interrogation of Jesus, and I asked Elena if this was what she found primitive. She pointed out that this is hardly an original device. Bulgakov had used it in his famous novel *The Master and Marguerita.* She had nothing against going back to classical themes. Russian novelists did it all the time. But she was not sure Aitmatov knew what he was doing. I pressed a bit more. I told her that some religious believers had told me they were outraged by Aitmatov's use of the gospel since he continues to describe himself as an atheist. She shrugged briefly, shook her head, and seemed to dismiss the issue. Still, she added, for many Russians the Aitmatov novel was an example of a superficial, even racy way of responding to the current upsurge of interest in theology. She thought something much more serious and engaging was needed and that we could confidently expect it in the future, maybe quite soon.

During the second cup of coffee, Elena told me about some conversations she had had with her husband, who had died two years before. It had become evident to her, she said, that, as he approached his death, something about the Orthodox tradition touched him immensely. He did not attend church, but he listened by the hour to tapes of the Orthodox liturgy for Eventide. After his death, she became curious about why that particular rite and its music had become so important to him. Eventually, she visited a monastery, attended the service, and then asked one of the monks to explain it to her. "And he did," she said. I waited, but she did not continue. Finally, when I asked what the explanation had been, she told me that, even though she could not repeat it now, it somehow satisfied her curiosity. It had helped her understand her husband's last days better.

Elena stirred her coffee and lit another cigarette. I could see she was uneasy. Had she sensed that we were touching on an area that would be awkward to pursue? Russians know that Westerners like explanations. But the schism between the aesthetic and the religious in the Western mind that Kierkegaard analyzed so vividly has never impressed the Orthodox very much. They know that an explanation that could satisfy them might not satisfy us. In any case, Elena seemed to want to shift the conversation to something a little lighter. She asked me brightly whether I believed churches should ever be locked. I told her that there was an old tradition that a church should always be open but that in many American cities they now had to be locked because of thieves and vandals. She nodded in an understanding way. She had, she said, occasionally tried to find a church in Moscow in which to sit, meditate, and perhaps pray during hours when no services were scheduled, but she had never found one.

The attempt to lighten the conversation did not last long. After a moment, Elena asked me if I had been wondering whether her husband thought of himself as a "believer." I had of course wondered, but I would never have asked. Well, she said, once a priest at a monastery he was visiting as a tourist offered to give him a blessing. He gladly accepted it, she said, but a few minutes later he went back to the priest and told him he thought he should know that he did not believe in God. The response of the priest, she said, was to smile, raise his hands palms up, and ask, "How can anyone know that for sure?" She paused again before going on. "I sometimes wonder whether I'm a believer, and the only answer I can give myself is, 'It all depends.' " She didn't elaborate, but I told her that I too was uncomfortable with people who divide the world so neatly between believers and unbelievers. She asked me to explain, so I said that every honest believer sometimes has doubts and that there were many atheists who sometimes doubted their unbelief. She listened intently and nodded, confirming my suspicion that the common parlance in Soviet society (and in America as well) that divides people between believers and nonbelievers has become less useful and less accurate. It does not do justice to the mixture of doubting, hoping, and searching that so many thoughtful people are grappling with today.

If Elena represented the seeker, "Dmitri," whom I met two evenings later, stood at the opposite end of the spectrum: he had found. An energetic man in his middle thirties, Dmitri had been raised in a strict Communist family, had belonged to the Komsomol, and had begun to have his doubts about Leninist dogma only during his years at the university. There, in part because of conversations with other students but also because he began to read nineteenth-century European philosophy, he found himself drifting out of the ideological stockade. He told me that his first "conversion" took him toward a kind of nineteenth-century German idealism. From there he said he moved toward Orthodoxy because he believed that Russian history had churned up all the basic and besetting issues of human life and that the religious tradition of his homeland had answered them in the most satisfactory way. More recently, he had embraced a stricter version of Orthodoxy, joining a congregation of Old Believers.

At first I was astonished to be talking to a living and breathing Old Believer. I knew the Old Believers' movement was the product of the "great schism" of the seventeenth century that erupted in response to the effort of Patriarch Nikon to rid the Russian Orthodox church of local accretions and to bring it more in line with the other Orthodox churches.

The Old Believers would have none of it. Eventually, many of their leaders were exiled to the most remote regions of the Russian Empire, but this only served, inadvertently, to spread their ideas further. Today, the Old Believers movement is still alive but is divided between congregations with duly ordained Orthodox priests who have chosen to serve Old Believers and a more sectarian group that has no priests and interprets the defection of the regular Orthodox priesthood as a sign of the Last Days. Dmitri belongs to the first, more moderate branch. But he insists that for him it is the only "true church," the one that has preserved unchanged and "unedited" the revelation of God in Christ and the authentic tradition that has flowered from it.

At first I found talking with Dmitri fatiguing, a little like trying to have a conversation with a particularly articulate Jehovah's Witness. Borrowing my pen, he drew a chart in the form of a tree rooted in the life of Christ with a long trunk and many branches. Most of the branches—which he scratched out by putting X's on them—were heresies, schisms, or errors; the true life of the tree could be found only at the top, in the Old Believers' version of Russian Orthodox Christianity. I nodded, and glanced at my watch. As we continued to talk, however, I slowly discovered that Dmitri was no fundamentalist. He was the best informed and most widely read of anyone I had talked with. He was the only Orthodox believer I met who was familiar with the German philosopher Martin Heidegger, whose writings he said he prized. He seemed positively impressed when he learned that I had studied with Paul Tillich, who had been influenced by Heidegger.

When I asked Dmitri why he felt sympathetic to Heidegger, he explained expansively. Heidegger, he said, had seen more clearly than any other European philosopher the gross error of modern technology and of modernity itself; he had called for a return to the original sources and had believed that most if not all of modern thought, including its theology, was a nest of mistakes. For Dmitri, this was a persuasive philosophy, but, as he pointed out, only in the Russian Orthodox church have an actual philosophy, theology, and culture been preserved from those times before the great modern apostasy he so deplored. Roman Catholicism and Protestantism, Dmitri went on, should be understood as no more than twin deviations that resulted from the fatal division of 1054, the year in which the break from the true Orthodox church became final. Just think, Dmitri concluded, with his arm raised for emphasis, without that split we would not have had the Roman errors that produced the Reformation, which Max Weber says gave rise to capitalism and all its corruption. We would all be so much better off. We would therefore not have communism, which emerged as a criticism of capitalism.

Dmitri had his own opinions. But he understood some of the issues of contemporary philosophy of religion quite well. Later, I discovered that he had organized a circle of discussants who met regularly in their Moscow apartments to argue about theological and philosophical themes in a kind of symposium atmosphere. He was anything but a closed-minded bigot. He told me that his great dream was to find a way to combine Christian theology with a Socratic method, one by which truth would emerge from the clash of honestly held positions. Religious thinkers in the world today, he lamented, were divided between dogmatists and relativists, and both these camps made genuine dialogue difficult. What point is there, he asked, in arguing with a relativist? As for him, he would rather argue with a good dogmatist any day, as long as the dogmatist was willing to converse.

Eventually, I asked Dmitri about the renewed interest in religion among Russian intellectuals. It was, he told me, inevitable. The collapse of Soviet Marxism as a credible philosophical system had left a gaping vacuum. University students now openly laughed at their professors of ideology. True, there were still some guardians of orthodoxy in the literary establishment who criticized the recent fascination with religion among intellectuals. He assured me, however, that almost everyone considered these thought censors to be a vanishing breed. No one took them seriously. For example, he told me, he himself works as an editor for a publishing house that prints mainly scientific texts, and his fellow editors view old-style Soviet ideology as little more than a joke. I asked him whether it would create any problems if his superiors knew he was a practicing believer. He smiled. If they ever asked him directly, he said, he would of course have to say yes. But he thought they never would—it would only create unnecessary embarrassment. Besides, everyone knew there would be no legal basis for dismissing him. Even the Soviet newspapers had recently taken to defending the legal rights of believers, so why should anyone bring it up?

For a moment or two, I considered asking Dmitri about the Aitmatov novel and its depiction of the Soviet Christ as trapped between two intransigent forces. But, after a moment's reflection, I decided not to risk it. I think he would have resented the depiction of the Orthodox church as a twin mastodon with the Communist establishment. He would certainly have a point. Mastodons, even though they are hampered by superfluous armor, are at least of roughly equal size and strength with other mastodons. The Orthodox church is hardly the equal of the vast state apparatus in the Soviet Union, and I quickly figured out that this is exactly why neither the seekers nor the finders I talked with felt comfortable criticizing it. The older ones had all lived through decades in which official state atheism and antireligious propaganda had pervaded the atmosphere. Our Western practice of freely criticizing the churches while we continue to be part of them has never taken root in Russian society, not just because Orthodoxy has never had either a reformation or a renaissance, but because it lives under a powerful government that is anything but neutral about religion. This history also in part explains why, when we talked about particular beliefs or doctrines, Dmitri always phrased his answer along the lines of, "We believe," or, "The Orthodox church teaches." He never once said, "I believe," or, "I think." When I finally asked him about his personal beliefs, he told me in friendly but firm tones that his faith was the faith of the church. It was not just his individual set of beliefs. He believed what the church believes. When I mentioned this some days later to another Russian friend, she smiled and told me that perhaps now I would understand a little better how all Russians think about most issues—in terms not of "I" but of "we."

Before we left the home of the friend in which we were talking, I had begun to feel quite warm toward Dmitri. What had begun as a sharp theological polemic had mellowed into a fraternal conversation, helped along perhaps by a small bottle of vodka I had bought in a hard currency shop. Still, just before we left, Dmitri smiled and assured me that, although it was clear we agreed on some things, there were still many others on which he was equally sure we disagreed and that we should start right away with them the next time we met. When I asked him what he thought the principle issue of disagreement might be, he shook his head and told me that I probably would have a lot of difficulty understanding the messianic role to which God had called the Russian people. I told him I might but that I wanted to hear more. He told me that he firmly believed God had chosen Russia both to continue the suffering that Christ had borne on earth and to preserve intact the gospel in all its richness and with all its traditional embellishments "unedited." He had used the word "unedited" before, and it now occurred to me that the fact that he worked in a publishing house might have influenced his choice of words. He also told me his reddish medium-length beard (unusual among present-day Muscovites) was an example of not "editing," of letting things, including a religious tradition, grow in a natural way. He assured me that this special calling of his own people did not reflect on the character, morality, or worth of any other nation. It was in fact a kind of burden that God had laid on Russians, like God's choosing the Jews. This was why, he explained to me, Russians never went into battle with the flourishes and heroics of some Western nations. War for Russians has always meant suffering, he said. We bear it willingly. We do not glory in it, but we recognize it sorrowfully as part of our calling.

It was close to midnight when Dmitri and the friend he had asked to interpret walked me to the taxi stand. As we waited for the cab, Dmitri talked on unabated. He suggested that, as someone who appreciates music, I surely knew the difference between the classics, the semiclassics, and pop tunes. I told him I thought I did. Well, he said, in one sense Orthodoxy represents the classical tradition. Orthodox Christians recognize that there will be other versions—elaborations, jazzed-up versions, and adaptations. Still, he suggested, someone has to continue to nurture the classics in their original form. Someone has to preserve high art, and it was the difficult—often thankless—task of Orthodoxy to do so. He was in mid-sentence when the taxi pulled up and I got in. He finished his last words, then smiled and closed the door for me. But, since the taxi was already pulling away during the final phrase, I can only guess what it might have been. It was probably something like, "You are mistaken, but God bless you," or words to that effect.

If Dmitri was the best informed and the most articulate of the new Christian intellectuals I met in Moscow, "Masha" was perhaps the most touching. Far from being a well-read or highly informed believer, Masha knew virtually nothing about the history and theology of Orthodoxy. Yet, in a society that still disapproves and sometimes makes life difficult for those who declare themselves to be believers, she does so openly. A poet, still largely unpublished at thirty-five, Masha met me in a friend's *dacha* just outside Moscow where she lives with her young daughter during the week and is joined by her husband on weekends. There in the cluttered kitchen or outside on a bench she writes her poetry and transcribes long passages of the works of recent Russian poets, especially those parts that have not yet been published but remain in underground, samizdat form. Far from considering this an irksome or laborious task, Masha, like some early Benedictine monk, seems to thrive on it. She loves to touch and transmit the words of the great poets. Meeting her reminded me of the singular place that poets hold in the hearts of all Russians, especially intellectuals. Poets are expected to be the prophets of the society, those who speak the truth and fearlessly call the people back to their moral vocation and spiritual anchorage. For Masha, copying their words is almost a spiritual exercise, and she did not complain about the task.

In her tiny unpainted hut equipped with a table and rough-hewn chairs, she also had an icon corner. The icons, however, were of the cheapest paper variety, available for a ruble in any monastery gift shop. Among hers were one of the Theotokos and one of Michael the Archangel, but the others represented obscure bishops and metropolitans whose names and faces I did not recognize. Masha seemed not to know much about them either. Apparently, having them on the wall was meant not to say much about these icons in particular, but about the tradition they represented and to which she felt so strongly drawn. Masha did not think of herself as an institutionally affiliated believer at all. She probably does not appear in any of the statistical tables. Nor was there anything of Dmitri's doctrinal assurance about her. She was desperately curious to find out from me all she could about the various religious traditions of the world and of the United States. What about Buddhists, Quakers, Baptists? What did Muslims believe about Christ? Unlike Dmitri, she voiced no criticisms and made no claims. For her, the Orthodox tradition was simply there. It was the one she turned to naturally as the principle resource for her spiritual life.

As we talked further, Masha told me that she worried constantly about the religious formation of her five-year-old daughter. She said that children learn nothing about God in the public schools and seemed surprised when in response to her questions I told her that there was also no religious teaching in the public schools of America. She asked about the availability of religious literature for children in the United States, and I told her that we had a lot, almost a surfeit of it, and that the problem was not finding it but selecting what was valuable out of all the junk. She looked incredulous. She had, she said, tried for years to get her hands on a Russian Bible, but they were virtually unavailable. She had rarely ever been able to see one, let alone have one to read. I told her the Soviet government had just announced that it was not against the publication and distribution of Bibles in principle but that the number available was restricted because of the limitations in paper and printing facilities. She waved her hand dismissively. She said she did not believe that story for a moment. We went on, but my mind kept going back to the unavailability of Bibles. How is the new generation of thoughtful Russians, now groping for an understanding of religion, to inform itself when even the most basic resources are so hard to lay hands on?

As we talked and drank tea, I noticed just to the right of the cluster of icons in Masha's corner a small picture of a man in an old-fashioned military uniform. When I asked her who it was, she smiled and explained that he was a general in the White Army during the civil war. I asked why she had him on her wall, and she smiled again. She had found the picture in the drawer of an old desk, she said, and had decided that putting it up was a way to tell herself and anyone who saw it about her lack of confidence in the Soviet society that had emerged from that civil war. She told me that sometimes the picture puzzled even her most dissident friends. Later, she showed me another cheap icon card that was not displayed but was lying with some papers on top of her small refrigerator. It showed what she called the "modern martyrs." I did not know who most of them were, but at the center I did recognize the familiar faces of Czar Nicholas II and his Czarina Alexandra, who were killed with all their children by the Bolsheviks in 1917. Still, it was hard to know whether Masha's religious commitment really included this somewhat heavy-handed preference for the old regime or whether she enjoyed being something of a nonconformist in the most available theological and political mode.

Masha wanted to continue to talk, but her daughter and a friend had appeared at the door in their bathing suits, carrying inflated inner tubes and demanding that she keep her promise to take them swimming. Still, she wanted my advice on how one could possibly raise these children to become believing Christians. I had only a moment or two to answer but told her I thought the most important thing was to tell them the stories. Make sure they knew about David and Ruth and Miriam and Jeremiah. Tell them about Jesus and his various encounters. These stories, I told her, would ultimately be more important for her children than the theological doctrines she might teach them. She nodded vigorously and seemed to agree but still looked at me in a puzzled way. As she disappeared down the path on the way to the pond, I began to understand her perplexity. How could she tell them the stories when she didn't know them herself?

The one non-Muscovite I talked with in my series of conversations was Kira, a Leningrader who had just finished her comprehensive exam in classical archaeology and was in Moscow to vacation and visit friends. Some of my new acquaintances told me she was terribly bright, so much so that she had gotten into the university without ever belonging to the Young Pioneers or the Komsomol. They also thought it would be important for me to talk to her since, at twenty-six, she would be the youngest of all my respondents. I phoned. She gladly agreed to talk and suggested that we meet one morning at the gigantic statue of Lenin in Octyabraskaya Square, a convenient location on the circle line of the Moscow subway system, about equidistant between her stop and mine. She said she was tall, had auburn hair, and described the clothes she would be wearing: faded blue jeans (almost de rigueur for Soviet youngsters today) and a maroon blouse.

I got on the subway at Leninski Prospect, and, when I climbed out at Octyabraskaya, I noticed that the little park around the Lenin statue seems to be a convenient place for many people to meet each other. It is just across the street from the Hotel Warsaw, two blocks from the hotel administered by the Soviet Academy of Sciences for overseas guests, and only a five-minute walk from the entrance to Gorky Park.

Kira arrived a few minutes after me and needed no encouragement to leap into the conversation. She is one of those young people who are at an exploratory stage, who are forming opinions on everything and do not mind sharing them with anyone who will listen. Sometimes these youthful opinions are silly or predictable, but Kira's were worth listening to, and her perspective on the return to spirituality in the Soviet Union provided a missing piece in my mosaic.

Kira came from a family of Orthodox believers who had never abandoned the faith but had become less open about it during the worst years of religious persecution. Only recently had they gone more public in their religious practice. She did not consider herself to be a recent convert in any sense of the word; rather, she was someone for whom Orthodoxy had always been. She was not "returning" to anything: she had always been there.

As we strolled along past the French embassy and the church of Saint Michael the Warrior toward the towers of the Kremlin churches ahead of us, Kira lost no time. She asked me about my own religious background, and, when I told her it was Baptist, she asked me with a facetious smile how we felt about the "filioque" controversy. Now I smiled. The Orthodox church believes this controversial word was inserted illegitimately into the Apostles' Creed by the Western church, thus providing one of the reasons for the Great Schism. I could not tell, however, whether Kira was asking me about the "filioque" as a kind of intellectual riposte, whether she had thought seriously about it, or whether it was a kind of an in joke. I decided to take the question seriously and explained to her that, although the filioque clause had admittedly been a divisive issue in the past, even the current pope has made some ameliorating remarks about it—and that there was little strong feeling on the subject one way or the other among my fellow Baptists. I did *not* tell her that most Catholics and Protestants in the West had never heard of it. When I had finished my answer, her smile broadened, and I sensed that in one way or the other I had passed my initial test.

As our conversation proceeded, however, it seemed to me that her Orthodox position on the filioque clause was hardly reflected in her other attitudes. She told me in no uncertain terms that she greatly preferred Gothic architecture to the Russian and Byzantine designs we were walking past. Although she had never been out of Russia and therefore had never visited Chartres or any of the other European cathedrals, she had obviously read about them and had perused pictures and paintings. Nor was her preference for things Western restricted to architecture. When the conversation turned to movies, she told me that her favorite film by far was *The Godfather* and that she found most Soviet films dull. She did make an exception for the recent Cannes special prize winner *Pokayaniye* (Repentance), directed by Tengiz Abuladze, which she thought was an important movie and one that was needed in order to continue to exorcize the Stalinist shadow. At the time I had not yet seen the movie because every screening in Moscow was sold out, but I knew that, next to the Aitmatov novel, it was causing the most discussion about religion. Set in a city in the Soviet republic of Georgia, the film deals with a Stalin-like figure named Varlam who is the mayor. In what could be an oblique lampoon of the Lenin cult or a reference to the episodic reappearance of Stalinism, Varlam keeps waking up after he is dead and rolling over to sleep more easily. But the central figures in the film are a young couple who are trying to prevent an old church from being turned into a factory. Eventually the young man, who physically resembles Jesus Christ, dies under torture in the gulag. But he too seems unwilling to die. One scene shows his face, uncovered in his grave in a dream sequence, his eyes wide open. The couple's daughter survives them and bakes tiny church-shaped cakes topped with little crosses. In the closing scene, an old woman asks her whether the street she is walking along leads to the church. The girl tells her it does not. The old woman then says, "What good is a street that doesn't take you to a church?" and limps determinedly away. Apparently, those words, appearing in a publicly exhibited Soviet film, have caused widespread puzzlement and debate. What did it mean? When I asked Kira, she shrugged. I asked if that was as far as one could go in such a public medium today—asking a strange question about religion. But, for once, Kira had no opinion. Were we now talking about something too important for hunches?

I asked Kira about her friends in the university and whether many of them were religious in any serious way. She told me there was such a trend but that in her view most people who followed it were "not serious." As it turned out, the phrase "not serious" was one Kira used often. She obviously wanted both to be a serious person and to be considered one, and she was predictably severe toward people who didn't—in her view— share that proclivity. For example, she could summon only a certain kind of disgust for the major animating passion of her fellow students at the university, which she claimed was devotion to different rock music groups. "Have you ever heard of Led Zeppelin?" she asked me. When I confessed that I had but not for a number of years, she told me that both that group and Pink Floyd were now immensely popular among her trendy university colleagues. She added further that there were the factions who supported rock, others who favored New Wave, and still others who went the way of Heavy Metal. She shook her head helplessly about what appeared to be the somewhat less than mature tastes of her fellow students.

Kira had heard about Aitmatov's book but told me she had absolutely no intention of reading it. "Aitmatov," she said, "is not really serious." He just played around with biblical symbolism and with Jesus and Pontius Pilate. It was all superficial. Lifting her eyebrows, she told me that in the novel, she had heard, "Aitmatov has Pilate's wife refer to him as 'Pontie.' " Apparently, for Kira this represented the nadir of bad taste and was further evidence of Aitmatov's lack of seriousness. I asked her if her main objection was that Aitmatov was not a believer. Yes, she said, it was. She told me that she thought Aitmatov had little business in fooling around with Christ and the apostles when he did not believe in God and could have no real feeling for what these figures meant to believers such as herself.

We walked along further. Suddenly, Kira suggested that we visit the Pushkin Gallery, a museum that has no Russian or Soviet section but exhibits exclusively Western art. I agreed, so we took another subway trip and came out at the Lenin Library stop, a few blocks from the Pushkin. This was clearly of a piece with Kira's other tastes. As we entered, she lovingly pointed out the Renaissance statuary and nineteenth-century French and Flemish painting as examples of the kind of art she strongly prefers. She told me that she loves to come to the Pushkin just to sit and read or write, surrounded by all that beauty. Then she looked at me directly and said that her most urgent hope in life was some day to be able to emigrate. As she grew older, she said, she recognized that she had no long-term affection or loyalty for Russia. She wanted to live somewhere else was the only possibility she could foresee, but she realized emigration might be difficult, even impossible. Still, she was even willing to postpone marriage for a few years to remain free for it rather than to complicate her chances.

When we left the Pushkin Gallery, Kira and I walked by the northern wall of the Kremlin and stopped to look at the towers of its churches with their bulbous golden domes glittering in the late afternoon sun. I told her I found it a breathtaking sight, but Kira was not impressed. She could not, she said, appreciate the Kremlin anymore: it had become "a toy." She thrust her hands in her pockets and, head down, stalked off in another direction. I was glad my friends had suggested that I talk with Kira. She was no Slavophile. For her, Orthodox religious faith was in no sense interchangeable with a deep affection for Russian culture. But she also resented, as any genuinely religious person does, the transformation of churches and sacred architecture into tourist displays, museums, and folklore. She of course blamed the trivialization of these monuments on Communism. I felt I should tell her that the same sad fate had overtaken many religious buildings and paintings in the West as well and that emigration, though it might solve some of her problems, would hardly solve that one. But I did not. Instead, I thanked her for the conversation and for the visit to the Pushkin Gallery and gave her as a token of my appreciation a T-shirt from the 1987 Boston Marathon. She beamed, stuffed it in her shoulder bag, and waved as her tramcar pulled away.

Two nights before I left Moscow, I had a conversation with "Alex," a forty-year-old performing musician. It turned out to be one of the most memorable and informative. A handsome man with a full beard, a heavy mane of hair, and sparkling eyes, Alex would have been a central casting dream for a nineteenth-century Russian peasant if it weren't for the modern Western suit coat and open-throated shirt he—and most other Moscow professionals—wore. Alex was the son of an Orthodox priest who is now living in semiretirement outside Moscow. He also told me that he still strongly identified himself as an Orthodox believer but that he had come to have many questions and felt that his search was far from over. In reminiscing about his childhood, he remembered that the hardest part about growing up in a strict Orthodox home in Soviet Russia was not that he felt discriminated against by official policies but that the spiritual regime enforced on the whole family by his father's vocation was so severe and difficult for a child to understand. The family had observed at least part of the monastic discipline of early morning prayers, prayers at eventide, and more prayers before going to bed, on a daily basis. Alex was also steered sternly away from such childhood pleasures as movies and card playing. As a normal young man, he had gone through a period of rebellion against his father's tutelage and had ceased practicing his faith. But he had never given up the core of Orthodox religiosity he had inherited from his parents. Yes, he said, he was a part of the return to religion among Russian artists and intellectuals, but unlike most of them he had something to return to, and he was glad.

Alex is an instrumental performer, but he also likes to sing and has a fine-quality, though untrained, tenor voice. He told me he enjoys singing in the choir of a small Orthodox church in the southern part of Moscow more than almost anything else. He sings there every Sunday and sometimes for Saturday vespers. He harbors no regrets that in Orthodox services the choir sings unaccompanied. He feels that it is one of the few places where the purity of the human voice can reach the heart unimpeded and unembellished by the organ or other artificial elements. Since we were sitting in the privacy of my apartment, I asked him if he wanted to sing. At first he declined, but later, after a glass of wine, he belted out a part of last week's liturgy. I could see why he loved it.

Like Masha, Alex wanted to talk about the difficulty he and his wife felt in raising their children as believers in Soviet society. He did not believe that official sanctions or administrative harassment provided the main problem. Rather, as in the West, parents had to watch their children absorb values and attitudes that seemed in direct conflict with Christianity. He talked about the fascination Soviet young people have for rock music, transistor radios, tape recorders, and the latest baggy blouses. He was afraid that both Soviet and Western societies were turning in a more materialistic direction and that this was making it difficult for the parents of young people to nurture them in the kind of Christian religious direction he and his wife wanted them to have. It was during this part of the conversation that Alex talked about the Soviet Baptists. It was one of the few extended remarks about them I had heard from any of my conversation partners, and I listened very carefully.

The people who study religion in the Soviet Union know that the number of Baptists is growing. There are sizable Baptist congregations in most of the large and medium size cities of the Soviet Union and numberless small congregations in the countryside. While I was in Moscow, I visited the First Baptist Church there and found nearly 2,000 people at a Sunday morning service. A young deacon told me that there would be two further services that day, one in the afternoon and one in the evening, mostly with different people in attendance, but each with a total of about 2,000 worshipers. During the service I attended, which lasted for nearly two hours, four different choirs sang, and we heard two sermons, both based on biblical passages. The sermons were a good corrective to the trivial bantering of American television evangelists. They dealt with death, destiny, suffering, the meaning of human life, and its purpose. There was no promise of pecuniary success showering on those who follow the way of the Lord. During the service, there were prayers for fellow Baptist congregations in Kiev, Odessa, and several smaller Soviet cities, congregations who were celebrating a special anniversary and had communicated the news to their Moscow brothers and sisters.

Alex was interested in the Baptists. He told me they were growing rapidly among less educated and less sophisticated people, and he thought it was too bad they had almost no contact with the Moscow intellectual community. But he did know a few Baptists, and he felt that as parents they had an advantage. They lived in a kind of religious subculture with other evangelical believers and therefore could supervise their children's nurturance better than cosmopolitan Muscovite intellectuals could. There was a certain wistfulness in his tone. But when I pressed him further about his views on the Baptists, he admitted that he could never embrace a version of Christianity that seemed to him too simplistic and that lacked any sense of liturgy or tradition. As he summed it up, in a phrase that seemed to say everything, "They have no icons."

Unlike Dmitri, my Old Believer friend, Alex could freely criticize and question many aspects of Orthodoxy without feeling that he was rocking a fragile bark. As a young man, he told me, after the tensions with his father had been settled, he read a good deal in Orthodox history and theology. He understood the reasons for the Great Schism of the seventeenth century that had produced the Old Believer's branch, and he also knew about the internal tensions of the Orthodox church during the Soviet period. He was aware of the connections between the Orthodox churches and the Western communions that are members of the World Council of

Churches. He believed that this was a good thing and that perhaps through the influence of the ecumenical movement the Orthodox church in Russia could be made more receptive to new ideas. Alex did not draw me any charts of Christian history, but I suspect that, if he had, Orthodoxy would have appeared as one branch among many.

I asked Alex about Aitmatov's novel with a certain amount of apprehensiveness. I was afraid he might feel like the other believers that it represented an intrusion or misuse of his faith. This was not the case. He told me that the biblical imagery and stories were the patrimony of a much larger group of people than those contained within any particular religious community and that a novelist should feel perfectly free to draw on them in telling his story. Alex seemed glad that the very existence of Aitmatov's book extended the boundaries of the current freedom of debate a little more. He did not feel that most secular intellectuals were doing their part to seize and enlarge this freedom. He talked in a particularly angry tone about one contributing editor to a well-known Soviet journal who had not objected when his most recent article had been "modified" for publication. Apparently, the writer had been so pleased with how much he *was* allowed to say, he felt that he should not press for more. But Alex disagreed with this strategy. He insisted it was important to use every opportunity to broaden and deepen the range of topics and opinions so that something like a genuine exchange of ideas, including ideas about religion, might eventually become possible.

As the evening wore on, we finished the bottle of French red wine I had bought at the diplomatic gastronome, and Alex became more sportive. He loosened his collar, he sang, he pretended to be addressing a listening device in the ceiling fixture and in the heating grate, which might not have been pretend at all since it was my apartment and most American guests expect their rooms to be bugged. He told two recent political jokes and one slightly salacious story that turned on a word play that I did not quite grasp. Then he got quite serious again. Recalling the question I had asked him earlier in the evening, about what Orthodoxy meant to him personally, he said he was now ready to answer and, reaching outward and upward, he traced a large semicircle in the air. "It's *ample,*" he said, "it's large. It can include everything. It gives us the widest imaginable horizon. It's not like the tiny, petty little ideas and theories and ideologies we're supposed to settle for." With these last words, he returned his arms from their extended position and hunched over to indicate miniscule little things with his fingertips.

By the time my visit to Moscow was ending, I had begun to realize that the way I had asked my questions might have sounded strange to my new acquaintances. I had hardly done justice to the singularity of their individual quests. I had not taken into sufficient consideration how much certain very old features of Russian culture—the suspicion of too much foreign influence, a sense of messianic vocation, the blending of beauty with holiness—still suffuse Soviet society today. My inquiry had left most of the large questions unanswered. For example, I wish I had asked someone to speculate on what would happen if, in the atmosphere engendered by *glasnost'*, books and journals touching on religious themes began to appear systematically? (Already, the editors of one such journal, bearing the title *Glasnost'*, are seeking approval for weekly publication.) What if such publications began reaching not just the intellectual elite but also the ordinary people? Will anyone be interested in them? Will the number of small study-discussion circles such as the one Dmitri organized begin to multiply? Will those circles get in touch with each other? If they do, how will that affect the present incipient religious awakening? It would not be the first time a major religious movement sprang from small groups meeting in homes. Remember the early Methodist "class meetings" and the present-day "Christian base communities" of Brazil. What will be the attitude of the Soviet government, which is now permitting the publication of an increased amount of literature that was once considered "subversive," toward believing parents who will certainly try to produce and distribute religious education materials?

Some of my questions had to do with the Orthodox church itself, which has often in its history discouraged both grass-roots initiatives and "foreign" religious influences. How will it cope with all this? Will it allow some *glasnost'* in the church itself? Will their widening contacts with theologians and churchpeople from other Christian traditions stimulate Orthodox leaders to reach out more energetically to the many thoughtful seekers one meets in the Soviet Union today? Or will the Russian Orthodox church become mainly a retreat into xenophobia? Is it too much to hope that the church in Russia might begin to nurture, if not a counterculture of art, drama, and poetry as the Roman Catholic church in Poland has, then at least an alternative to the official Soviet culture, which everyone from Gorbachev down concedes is stagnant? On the other hand, what would happen to the religious stirrings if Gorbachev, as his enemies hope and his supporters fear, goes the way of Khrushchev or is simply defeated by bureaucratic inertia and *immobilisme?*

On my last day in Moscow, I decided to pay a farewell visit to what had become my favorite spot, the small and somewhat overlooked little chapel inside the Kremlin walls called the Church of the Deposition of the Robe. It was there that Yuri had first seen me, and I had gone back a couple of times since then. Overshadowed by the much more impressive cathedrals, this tiny church is sometimes missed or ignored. Centuries ago, it served as the private chapel of the patriarch and then of the czars and their families. Like all Orthodox churches, its main altar is shielded by an iconostasis covered with ranks of icons. On this particular screen, however, there is an unusual feature: one whole rank is devoted to the life of Christ, beginning with the Annunciation and Nativity and ending with the Resurrection and the scene on the road to Emmaeus. In looking at this iconostasis, I noticed that the one event in the whole life of Christ between his Dedication at the Temple and the Triumphal Entry that seemed worthy of depiction to those who painted it was that of Christ raising Lazarus from the dead. There were no teaching scenes, no Sermon on the Mount, no healings; only the powerful image of the Savior calling forth life from death.

The raising of Lazarus plays a powerful role in the history of Russian religious faith. For Dostoevski it represented the miracle of faith itself. In *Crime and Punishment,* he pictures Sonia reading about it to Raskolnikov:

> She was trembling in a real physical fever. . . . She was getting near the story of the greatest miracle and a feeling of immense triumph came over her. Her voice rang out like a bell; triumph and joy gave it power. The lines danced before her eyes, but she knew what was she was reading by heart. At the last verse, "Could not this man who opened the eyes of the blind . . ." dropping her voice she passionately reproduced the doubt, the reproach and censure of the blind disbelieving Jews, who in another moment would fall at His feet, as though struck by thunder, sobbing and believing. . . . "And he—he, too—is

> blinded and unbelieving, he, too will hear, he, too will believe, yes, yes! At once, now," was what she was dreaming, and she was quivering with happy anticipation.

Sonia's quivering anticipation as she read the story sprang from the hope that its sheer power and beauty would surely touch even the unbelieving heart of Raskolnikov. He too, by the power of this Russian Christ, should be called from the death of skepticism and contempt into the joyful life of faith. Such at least was Sonia's faith.

As I stepped out of the darkness and silence into the brick Kremlin square next to the czar's bell, surrounded by clumps of chattering tourists from the Soviet hinterlands, it occurred to me that the Church of the Deposition of the Robe had helped me understand my conversations with my new friends. Ivan's priest was at least partly right. Though they may not teach us all we need to know, "the icons teach us." I could also understand Masha's and Elena's feeling that the music and liturgy of Orthodoxy bring something to the human spirit that penetrates deeper than ideas. I could understand Dmitri's reluctance to allow any of this to be watered down by relativism or adaptation. Mostly, I could almost hear Kira's voice when, thinking of that overwhelming iconostasis, I said to myself, "This is serious."

The search for a Soviet Christ is surely underway. I have no wisdom on whether it will succeed, even on what success in such a quest would be. I doubt that Masha or Dmitri or Ivan even think much about the success of their venture. Their search for mystery and meaning—for God—is shaped to some extent, as it is for anyone, by the contours of the culture they live in. But the search also leads to something that is, to use Alex's words and gestures, larger and more ample. But I did decide one thing: the search for a Soviet Christ will never go anywhere unless it deals with the Russian Christ, that resolute figure who gazes mournfully but serenely from the icons. To know him would not be easy in any society, and, although under *glasnost'* the possibility that the quest will succeed is less remote, it is not any less difficult.

7

Beyond Dialogue: Liberation Theology and Religious Pluralism

There can be little doubt that the plurality of religions in one small globe poses a major question to Christianity today. Can we summon the theological resources to respond to it? The answer is not immediately clear. The most vigorous theological current today is liberation theology. But because it centers so emphatically on Jesus and the promise of the reign of God—both of which can be interpreted as highly particularistic Christian motifs—many people believe liberation theology has little to contribute to interfaith dialogue. Some of its critics even contend that liberation theology is one further example of Western religious imperialism. Is this an accurate assessment of the situation?

For the last decade I have divided my theological reflection into roughly two areas. I have spent half my time learning about liberation theology, particularly in Mexico, Brazil, and Nicaragua; and the other half studying and taking part in the interfaith dialogue that took me to Japan and India. As a result of this work my own hunch is that liberation theology is not only compatible with a rich interfaith encounter but that it has a distinct contribution to make to this dialogue which might move it beyond its present stalemate.

Let me begin with the undeniable religious heterogeneity of the dawning postmodern world. Not only do we live on a spiritually multiplex globe, but nearly every continent, nation, and city is itself increasingly pluralistic. As a result of nineteenth-century Christian missionary activity, worldwide migration patterns, and the spread of Asian religious practices in the West, previous "spheres of influence" arrangements no longer work. Everyone is now everywhere. There are native-born Presbyterians in Cambodia; third-generation Buddhists in the United States; and Hindu temples in the Caribbean. Ghetto religions—those that rely on an element of isolation to survive—are dying out. Hare Krishnas chant in Saint Peter's Square in Rome; Christianity is reappearing in China; and young Indian untouchables calling themselves "panthers" recently began converting to Buddhism to escape the Hindu caste system. Religions now coexist and interact whether or not theologians or mullahs or bishops approve. Religious pluralism is an irreducible fact.

It is also true that liberation theology, insofar as it springs from a Latin American background, is limited by the relative religious uniformity of its home continent. Unlike Africans or Asians, South American Christians have not had to deal over the centuries with the vigorous presence of "rival" religions since indigenous Indians and enslaved Africans were restricted to the margins of society and in any case often accepted Christianity as their own. At first glance, liberation theology does not seem particularly well suited to deal with religious pluralism, and until quite recently has not done much to overcome this limitation.

In modern academic theological circles, however, the picture is quite different. In the past decade religious pluralism has emerged as the most debated question of all. Page through the titles of the articles published in the most influential journals of theological and religious studies for the past ten years. Glance at the catalogs of books on religion rolled out by the presses. Look at the course offerings in seminaries and college religion departments. Sometimes one gets the impression that religious pluralism is the only thing worth talking about. Nor is it merely something tacked on or restricted as it once was to "comparative religion" courses. It is changing nearly every field of religious study. Instead of emphasizing the uniqueness of the ancient Hebrew faith, Old Testament scholars search for parallels with the Canaanites. Once viewed as peripheral, the gods of the Syrians and the Babylonians are now studied sympathetically. New Testament students compare the Pauline Epistles and the synoptic Gospels with gnostic scrolls and Buddhist or Hindu texts. Students of ethics have become fascinated with the moral exemplars and law codes of other religious traditions. Philosophers of religion ransack Western and Asian texts for universal values. Scholars investigate the comparative psychology of religion, the comparative phenomenology of religion, and comparative spiritual practices.

But if liberation theology has a problem with religious pluralism, so does academic theology. One can compare and contrast religions only up to a point. The people who study religion are not ciphers. They are faced with the same questions of life and death and right and wrong with which the various religions deal. They cannot avoid the question of truth forever. Economists who investigate rival theories of savings and inflation must decide how to invest their own money. Students of comparative religion eventually have to decide how they are going to live their lives and make their decisions. They have to ask what faith, if any, will guide their ultimate choices. This unavoidable need to choose has pushed the academic study of religion toward a frank acknowledgment that no one can study religion merely descriptively. This in turn makes the modern myths of neutrality and objectivity increasingly implausible.

Whatever else one might say about them, liberation theologians have never thought that the study of other religions could be neutral. They see something terribly important at stake, the salvation of persons from bondage and the liberation of captives from oppression. Ironically, the momentum of current academic studies in religious pluralism is pushing it toward an approach that is similar to liberation theologies. In fact, liberation theologies might even help the academic study of religion find a way out of its current cul-de-sac.

Modern theologians are beginning to realize that they have reached a certain crossroads in the study of world religions. In the spring of 1982, after spending a number of years examining the confusing welter of literature that has appeared on this topic during the past decade, a scholar named Carl Raschke attempted to make some sense out of the babble. Raschke realized that the question of the diverse claims to truth made by the different traditions would finally have to be faced.

Raschke lists four ways students of religion deal with the "truth question." The first is the so-called phenomenological approach. It stresses a careful and sympathetic study of the various expressions of faith by a method that tries not just to observe but to feel its way into their singular and concrete reality. This method assumes that one should listen without preconception since what people actually believe is often not what the theologians say they should. The various faiths are studied without making any judgments about their validity or truth.

This first approach requires a certain mixture of attention, caring, and suspension of judgment. It is equally applicable whether one is sitting in a serpent-handling church in West Virginia, swaying with the devotees in a Krishna temple in Vrindavan, listening to the chanting of Tibetan monks, or pondering an opaque Talmudic text. It is not the cool, objective detachment of analytical observation. What is required by this method is a trained capacity for entering in, listening to, and watching without evaluating. It is a method most American undergraduates take to almost instinctively.

The trouble with this listening and feeling approach is that, before long, anyone investigating faith confronts issues of life and death. It is one thing to appreciate at some depth why thirteen-year-old Iranian boys walk into Iraqi minefields secure in the belief that if they are blown to bits they will be rewarded by Allah with eternal life. But religious faith by its very nature has to do with the things one will live and die for; so the question, Is it true? inevitably arises.

The second route Raschke registers is also familiar to me since it has come to be associated with my colleague Professor Wilfred Cantwell Smith, former director of the Center for the Study of World Religion at Harvard. Wilfred Smith's highly original contribution is often capsulized with the phrase "one doesn't study 'religions,' one studies people." Even the word "religion," he says, is itself a misleading abstraction. For Smith, what one should study is "faith." And faith can be found only in humans and in the traces they leave in rite, scripture, and custom. For Smith, faith is that great confidence and joy that alone enables human beings to feel at home in the universe. It is what permits them to find meaning both in the world and in their own lives. Furthermore, this confidence must be sufficiently deep so that—unlike a belief or an opinion or an idea—it remains stable no matter what happens at the level of immediate events.

Wilfred Smith wants the method to be more than descriptive. He believes that, when religious men and women discard abstractions like Buddhism and Christianity and deal honestly with themselves and each other as creatures of faith, a certain "convergence" is bound to occur. They sense a common source of confidence. Smith has never succeeded in showing how such a convergence happens. Expecting this convergence may itself be a matter of faith, something that, along with Professor Smith, one can hold to and hope for but cannot demonstrate to "those of little faith." This approach too falls short of providing any way to confront the question of truth.

The third approach, according to Raschke, is exemplified by those scholars who contend that behind the infinite particularities of the various expressions of faith there lies a single primordial tradition. This primordial tradition is not readily visible, but it is there. It is the underlying stratum of which the separate "religions" of the world are so many surface stalagmites, and it can be uncovered by the careful geologist of faith. Religious thinkers in this school view Christianity and the other traditions as variants of something larger and more comprehensive—God's inclusive revelation to all creatures or the universal human capacity for religiousness.

This unity-behind-the-diversity position is widely held among both scholars and lay people. One clear expression of it is that of Professor John Macquarrie of Oxford University. Taking a philosophical approach, Macquarrie sees the riddle of religious pluralism as analogous to the age-old debate about "the one and the many," an argument that goes back at least to the ancient Greeks. "God," for Macquarrie, is the name of the ultimate unity beyond all seeming contradictions and differences. He writes, "These religions will be living side by side on earth in the foreseeable future. They must seek to draw more closely together and demonstrate by common life and action their fundamental commitment to the One, however that One may be named in each religion. . . . No single faith has yet attained to the understanding of the fullness of the One. . . . Therefore each faith must be respectful and ready to learn from the spiritual insights of others."

Raschke describes this correctly as a "Hindu solution" to the question of pluralism. It claims, in effect, that the variegation in religious traditions is only a secondary quality, that underneath all the separate rivers and rivulets of faith draw on a single mighty reservoir. All the gods are avatars of the divine reality.

Again, as we saw with Wilfred Smith's confidence in the "convergence" of persons of faith, this third position may be true, but it is not demonstrably true. Like Smith's hope, this vision of an unseen unity also requires a considerable leap of faith. In this case, however, the leap is into a faith that would be much more acceptable to an educated modern Hindu whose tradition already posits a single divine source with a million faces than it would to most Muslims or Orthodox Jews. It would appeal to the mystical strains in the world's religions (Sufism, esoteric Buddhism, gnostic Christianity) but not to their more orthodox branches. All this does not mean this approach is not true. It means only that it postulates a certain answer (a "Hindu" one) before the other alternatives are carefully investigated.

Finally, Raschke discusses a fourth method of dealing with pluralism, one advocated by the Indian Catholic Raimundo Panikkar. It is a form of dialogue among persons of different faiths, but it is not the kind of dialogue that focuses on the differences and/or similarities among religious traditions. What Panikkar advocates is a dialogue that draws partners into the "unspoken center" they share.

For Panikkar, a priest and mystic whose father was a Hindu and whose mother was a Spanish Roman Catholic, most dialogues between religious persons go astray when the participants begin advocating, comparing, defending, conceding—like diplomats negotiating a treaty. What Panikkar yearns for is more respect for silence, more shared awe and ecstasy. One neither hides the differences nor trumpets the similarities but allows both to be what they are. One waits and listens. The procedure is a nonviolent one, reminiscent of Gandhi's *ahimsa*.

Clearly, all the methods Raschke mentions for confronting the dilemma of religious pluralism have their strengths. But when one adds them all up, the question of truth is still missing. Raschke recognizes this. He suggests that it is time for both the study of religion and the dialogue among religious persons to be taken out of the sphere of description and comparison. Those engaged in the activity must recognize that there is another dimension, that the reality to which their words and silences point must also become a part of the process itself. Dialogue must cease to be secondary reflection about religion and become itself a religious quest. When this happens, he believes dialogue will also become an occasion for further revelation, a new disclosure of the divine.

Raschke thinks that the course he is advocating will carry us "beyond theology." He even suggests coining a new word, "dialogy," to make the change clear. True, the path he suggests will take us beyond modern theology and beyond modern religious studies as well, but must it take us beyond theology as such? For Raschke the answer is yes because for him theology inevitably entails what he calls "circumscribing the divine as an object of reflection" whereas dialogy "cuts through all standard representations" in order to "let the ancient runes speak." Raschke is afraid theologies are already too jelled, too fixed, and that therefore even a cross-cultural theology will remain at the level of mingling and sorting existing traditional connotations: nothing new can happen. Dialogy would bring these beliefs into "interpretive tension" and "relax their iconic rigor" so that one becomes aware of multiple layers of meaning.

By "dialogy" does Raschke mean something close to what some call "postmodern theology"? He might not agree that he does, but this may be because of his conception of theology as a static way of thinking, one whose boundaries are already firmly nailed down. But what if theology were not as graven in stone as he thinks it must be? Evidence that it is not is coming from a variety of directions, but especially from what I call "The edges and the bottom." The Chinese Christian theologian C. S. Song, writing in what a Japanese colleague calls a "post-First-World Age" vein, gently suggests that God suffers and feels the pain of human beings. From El Salvador, Jon Sobrino shows that a God who loves actually and not just figuratively must be wounded and hurt just as the people in whom God dwells are hurt. Isabel Carter Heyward, a daring feminist theologian, suggests not only that God is changing and becoming but that God's entering into real give-and-take with human beings means that human beings actually contribute to the redemption of God.

In the final analysis it does not matter if the postmodern theologies now arising are called "theology" or "dialogy" or something else. What is important is that Christians meet their fellow human beings of the other great religious traditions not in a detached or aggressive way but with a willingness to listen together to what the ancient runes say. It is important that this mutual listening take place not in some demarcated religious sphere but in the day-to-day combat and compromise of life. The inner logic of the strictly academic approach to religious pluralism is leading it out of the academy and into the grimy world, in which liberation theologies are also trying to cope with the same cacophony. But how well are they doing so far?

Most Latin American liberation theologians ignore the issues of religious pluralism. The Hispanic Catholic tradition is pervasive on the South American continent, and they have been relatively blind (until recently) to indigenous and African religions there. But liberation theologians and grassroots communities in other parts of the world, especially in Asia, have begun to tackle the issue, and it is to them we now turn. The liberationist approach to religious pluralism comes from politically committed Christians in those sections of the world where pluralism is not merely an intellectual question but also a political one and a fact of everyday life. It has started among Christians who have come into close contact with revolutionary movements in regions where issues of injustice and class confrontation are interwoven with those of caste, religion, and communal loyalties.

Tissa Balasuriya is a Roman Catholic priest from Sri Lanka, the country Westerners used to call Ceylon. As an Asian, he lives in a part of the world where Christian churches exist as tiny minorities. He also lives in a region that has felt the full impact of European colonial control and the erosive power of Western business enterprises, both emanating from allegedly Christian continents.

As an Asian Christian, Balasuriya says he welcomes Latin American liberation theology as a long-needed break from the dominant role played by European and North American theologians. For many years these theologians have provided the agenda for theologians everywhere without being fully aware of how much the Western context in which they lived, that of capitalist affluence, tinctured what they wrote. As a Sri Lankan who is committed to the ongoing attempt by those who suffered from the colonial heritage to begin again, Balasuriya also welcomes liberation theology as a contribution to the actual liberation process.

As an Asian himself, however, Balasuriya also has some criticisms of Latin American liberation theology. He has voiced them frequently as the theological interaction between Asia and Latin America has been stepped up in recent years. The Latin Americans' concentration on the relatively recent history of capitalist expansion as the historical form of social sin leads them, he believes, to overlook the longer history of white European expansion, a process driven by more factors than economic ones. He believes this oversight explains the failure of Latin American theologians to express much concern about the monstrous destruction of the Maya, Aztec, and Inca civilizations that were flourishing before the arrival of the Spanish. He also asks why nearly all Latin American theologians (like the secular ruling circles within Latin America) are lighter skinned and of European origin while the poorest people are of Indian or black African descent. Balasuriya believes there is a religious, cultural, and racial blind spot in Latin American liberation theology, and this is a point on which he is supported especially by some North American black theologians.

Balasuriya's criticism raises some troubling issues. Is there somewhere within Christianity itself, not just in its modern form, a defective gene that propels it into periodic outbursts of ruthless expansion, of crusades, pogroms, and conquests, at the expense of other people's cultures? If not, is there a quirk that makes Christianity susceptible to being used by expansionist or dominating secular movements? Why has it been possible for the so-called Great Commission ("Go ye into all the world and preach the gospel") to be exploited time and again by imperial forces bent on conquest and rapine rather than on love or service? Does this proclivity stem from the church's early entanglement with the Greek idea of *paideia,* the responsibility of the Hellenes to "civilize" barbarians? This would make the flaw more a malformation resulting from an infantile trauma than a genetic one: serious but not fatal. Was the "religionizing" of the message of Jesus itself an error that for millennia has unnecessarily divided Christians from people whose lives have been shaped by what the modern world calls "religions" (a concept itself invented—as we have just seen in Wilfred Smith's work—by the Christian West)? Without denying that it has allowed itself to be flagrantly misused by a money-obsessed system that contradicts its inner essence, the hard question remaining is whether there is something in Christianity as a "religion" that makes it susceptible to this perversion. If there is such a defective gene or quirk, then Balasuriya is right: the scale and scope of the theological changes needed are much larger than those that most liberation theologians presently envisage. Only a serious dialogue between Christians and people from religious traditions that have not exhibited this expansionist obsession, at least not as egregiously, will enable us to answer these questions.

Balasuriya believes Latin American liberation theology would be greatly strengthened if it took more seriously both the spirituality of its own indigenous populations and the experience of the world religions. He knows the narrow focus of Latin American theology is in large measure simply the result of a history that spread Catholic Christianity across and entire continent. "But," he says,

> in many other parts of the world the struggle for human liberation has to take place within the context of pluralistic societies. Hence the action-reflection groups and even the "grassroots communities" would be not only of Christians but also of believers of other religions such as Hinduism, Buddhism, Islam, Confucianism, etc. The "revision of life" then would have to be based on a much wider inspiration drawn from different traditions including a deeper understanding of the human person, of the world and of the Absolute. This would involve a wider form of ecumenism than is generally met in Latin American theological reflection.

This "wider ecumenism," Balasuriya believes, would have far-reaching implications for mission and evangelization. It is important to recognize that for this Asian Christian it would not mean a watering down of the gospel so as to make it more acceptable to Buddhists or Hindus. Rather, he sees an Asian liberation theology celebrating a "cosmic Christ" who is present in all cultures and religions as well as being the (more "Western") Lord of history. Thus Asian liberation theology has begun to address the vexing issue of religious pluralism, the same question that exercises the academy so much. But again, one should not be misled by superficial similiarities. There is a vast difference between the academic and the liberationist approaches to religious pluralism.

Liberation theology rejects the notion that there can be any neutral theology or any detached understanding of who Jesus was and is. This means that significant thinking about Jesus can go on only among people who are seriously following Jesus—that is, trying to make Jesus' life purpose their own. The purpose of Jesus' life was the coming of the kingdom of justice and peace, of which he was himself the chief exemplar. Hence, the struggle for the reign of divine justice provides the only appropriate context within which any meaningful discussion about Jesus can go on.

Balasuriya and his liberationist colleagues have a point. Arguments about the significance of Jesus ("Christology") have always been political as well as theological. The various titles and interpretations of Jesus—Messiah, Son of Man, the Pantocrator of the Hagia Sophia, the bleeding Man of Sorrow—were not invented in seminars but came out of a contentious and conflict-ridden human history. At the scene of the crucifixion itself a dispute broke out among the priests and the Roman officials about what should be written on the sign above the Cross. The argument continues today. The centuries-long battle over how to answer the question, "Who do you say I am?" is in part a debate between those who want to control the meaning of Jesus because they recognize his political significance all too well. We can understand and evaluate these different images—such as the "historical Jesus" or the "cosmic Christ"—only as we recognize the politics of Christology and only as we participate in that same history.

This point about the ongoing political history of Christology is also crucial in contending with religious and cultural pluralism. The struggle for the coming of the kingdom provides the context for the "wider ecumenism" Balasuriya calls for. As he sees it, this context includes people who are not Christians. The argument about who Jesus was is also about who he is. It is inseparable from the question of what the reign of God means and how and where it is appearing today. These discussions did not stop with the Gospels, the Apostle's Creed, the "classical Christologies," or more recent reformations. The important point is not only that the discussion goes on but that it proceeds within history, not above it.

For liberation theology the principal objective of Christological thought is not to ascertain whether a particular image of Christ comports with one of the orthodox confessions. It is to determine how a given formulation actually contributes to the coming of the kingdom, and this is a question to which people other than Christians can contribute. Words mean different things at different times and in different settings. The same Christological title that once clarified the meaning of Jesus and signaled the coming of the New Era can now distort his original meaning. Therefore, theologians must always ask how, by whom, and for what purposes various Christological images are used. The most difficult continuing critical task of Christology is to prevent the misuse of ideas about Jesus to thwart his purpose, stifle his emancipatory message, and control the people among whom he was and is opening God's reign.

What I have sketched here is not an answer to Balasuriya's question about a "cosmic Christ." It is a description of how liberation theologians might go about addressing such a question. It not only asks the ancient runes to speak again; it asks them to speak in such a way that they are heard by the outsiders and the brokenhearted as a word of hope and freedom.

What the various liberation theologies make clear is that any dialogue about Christ and his significance must proceed today in an era characterized by both religious pluralism and class strife. The question of who Jesus is and how the reign of God can be interpreted in a religiously plural world is a political as well as religious question. It can be answered only by women and men who see the gospel not as one religious tradition among others—to be compared, defended, synthesized—but as a call addressed primarily to all the rejected and outcast peoples of the world, whatever their cultural or religious tradition. Perhaps we can clarify how liberation theology can contribute to the great debate about religious pluralism by going back for a moment to the different routes Carl Raschke describes. Liberation theology uses all of them, but in every instance it does so by placing the religious dimension in its larger political and cultural setting.

Liberation theologians like Balasuriya are, in some ways, "phenomenologists." They try not to make dogmatic judgments about Buddhists or Hindus. They try to enter their worlds with empathy. But the mode of their entry is guided by the Kingdom idea; they do so as Jesus did, by taking the side of the lowest castes, the outsiders, the poor, and the ritually impure.

As in the second stance Raschke mentions, the one associated with Wilfred Cantwell Smith, liberationists are also more concerned with people than with "religions." However, they are most concerned with particular people, the hurt and the helpless, the despised classes.

Like the scholars of the third approach who look for a hidden transcendental unity in all particular faith expressions, the liberationists also envision a world in which unjust divisions and racial and class hatred will be abolished. But for the liberationist this unseen reality lies ahead, not beneath or behind. It is eschatological, not primal. It requires faithful love and service, not esoteric insight.

Finally, along with Raimundo Panikkar, liberation theologians reject the idea that one can gain any value by merely reflecting on and comparing theological formulations. New insight comes only through reflective action.

For the majority of the world's Christians, most of whom are poor or colored and many of whom live among men and women of different faiths, the liberation approach to religious pluralism is already a great liberation. It is a relief not to have to enter into theological debate with every Muslim or Sikh or Buddhist before deciding whether to cooperate in the combat against social evil and in the celebration of the promise of life. In story after story and teaching after teaching Jesus insists that God gives the Kingdom to the poor because they have nowhere else to turn, not because of their doctrinal orthodoxy or moral purity. He teaches that God extends the reign to anyone who is willing to accompany the poor in their efforts to claim that Kingdom against those who withhold it from them.

In the light of this "Kingdom-centered" view of Christology, the whole meaning of the discussion with people from other religious traditions shifts. The purpose of the conversation is different. Interfaith dialogue becomes neither an end in itself nor a strictly religious quest but a step in anticipation of God's justice. It becomes praxis. Similarities and differences that once seemed important fade away as the real differences—between those whose sacred stories are used to perpetuate domination and those whose religion strengthens them for the fight against such domination—emerge more clearly.

For Christians, the theological basis for this shift in the nature of the interfaith dialogue is not so hard to find. When the disciples reported to Jesus that they had discovered individuals they did not even know freeing people from demons and asked him if they should not do something about it, Jesus quickly assured them that it was what these people were doing and not how they were interpreting it that was important: "He who is not against me is for me." At another time Jesus insisted that verbal definitions of who is "for or against" the coming of the Kingdom are secondary at best. He praised the brother who obeyed his father's command—even when he said he would not—rather than the brother whose obedience was a matter of words. Later Jesus warned his followers that not everyone who says "Lord, Lord" receives grace, but only those who do God's will. Pagans, Samaritans, prostitutes, and publicans inherit the Kingdom. The orthodox priests and temple rulers trail along later.

In the face of these clear warnings from Jesus himself it seems difficult to justify any form of interreligious dialogue in which the poor are systematically excluded. The favored format for most dialogues today is one in which representatives of the various religious traditions of the world—usually scholars or ecclesiastical leaders whose positions make them more attuned to confessional than to class differences—meet and converse about what unites or separates them. But it is the hard reality of social conflict, not just exchanging ideas, that creates unity or foments division. Christians who have participated with Hindus and humanists and others in actual conflict against the powers that be "do theology" in a different way. They do it as part of an emerging worldwide community made up of the despised and rejected of the modern world and their allies. In this new community, as in those tiny first-century congregations of ex-slaves and day workers in Colossae and Ephesus where they had also begun to hear the same good news, the most intransigent of religious, traditional, and cultural barriers no longer have the power to divide. Those earliest followers of Jesus took a decisive step "beyond dialogue." With the help of liberation theology, perhaps we can do the same today.

8

"The Heart of a Heartless World": Christians and Marxists Examine Religion

My first job after completing my Ph.D. in religion at Harvard in 1962 was in Berlin. By means of a complex set of arrangements I was sent to work for one year as an "Ökumenische Mitarbeiter"—usually translated in English as "Ecumenical Fraternal Worker." I was paid by American Baptists; assigned by the World Council of Churches to the Protestant church of Berlin-Brandenburg (then still presided over by the aging Bishop Otto Dibelius); placed at the disposal of a kind of lay theology institute called the Gossner Mission that had centers in both East and West Berlin; and then actually posted in Gossner's East Berlin program on the "other side" of the bricks and barbed wire. I was supposed to take part in the "Marxist-Christian dialogue" which was then in its earliest stages.

It was a memorable year. Thanks to the mysterious intricacies of the Four Power Agreement by which Berlin was then governed, I was allowed to travel through the wall to the East Sector from my residence in the Friedenau district of West Berlin, by way of Checkpoint Charlie on a daily basis since I held an American passport. I just had to be sure to return to the West every day before midnight. To make matters a little more complicated, Pastor Bruno Schottstadt, who then headed the Gossner Mission's operation in East Berlin, thought that in addition to teaching in the Lay Theological Education program I should also attend the weekly meetings of Unterwegs Ost ("On the Way East"), a lively theological discussion group consisting of East German pastors and teachers, and also serve as a part-time staff member at the Protestant Academy in East Berlin. All in all I spent the year as a commuter between two worlds which at that time seemed far more divided than they do in these latter days of *glasnost'* and *perestroika*.

During that year in a broken city I learned two important things about Marx and Marxism. The first was that Marx himself, whose works I had to study assiduously in order to carry out my assignment, was a truly impressive thinker whose ideas about religion were far more nuanced and complex than I had thought they were. I am not a Marxist, but since that year of massive exposure to his ideas, both in his books and through people I met, I have never been able to dismiss him as easily as some scholars who, I suspect, have read very little Marx and never met a real Marxist.

The second thing I learned, however, from dwelling in the shadow of the Wall, was to look with unswerving suspicion on those who make Marxism into a dogmatic orthodoxy or a ruling ideology. I returned from Berlin with a profound respect for Karl Marx's ideas and an equally profound contempt for the people who placed his picture on billboards overlooking barbed-wire barriers and guard towers.

In the twenty-five years that have passed since I returned from Berlin something quite curious has happened. Maybe because the appeal of Marxism as a philosophy of life has declined, fewer and fewer people seem interested in a "Marxist-Christian dialogue." But at the same time Christian theologians have begun utilizing certain Marxist methods in their work, and Marxists have drastically altered their once dogmatic rejection of religion as a mere "opiate of the masses." The use of modes of analysis derived from Marxism is not confined to liberation theologians. It is also employed, along with a variety of other methods, by biblical scholars, church historians, and ethicists. I am finding this approach useful myself. But how can the thought of someone who has become the most famous atheist in history help us understand religion?

There is no single Marxist theory of religion. There are many. Still, in setting forth the essential elements of Marx's own approach, one good place to start is with the locus classicus in his *Contribution to a Critique of Hegel's Theory of Right,* where this famous paragraph appears: "Religious distress is at the same time the *expression* of real distress and the *protest against* real distress. Religion is the sigh of the oppressed creature, the heart of a heartless world, just as it is the spirit of a spiritless situation. It is the *opium* of the people."

Ordinarily, readers of Marx have singled out the last—and most notorious—phrase of this paragraph, "the *opium* of the people." But what about the characterization of religion as "the sigh of the oppressed creature" and "the heart of a heartless world"? In my opinion, the "opium" sentence has been misused by disparagers of Marx, most of whom know little of the context in which it appears. The phrase, however, is useless as a real index of Marx's complex attitude toward religion. The other metaphors, "sigh" and "heart," are much more suggestive.

Would it help us to understand the religious rituals and beliefs of a people if we view them—in part at least—as "sighs," as expressions of their deepest fear and pain? Dorothy Soelle says in her book *Suffering* that a movement from "muteness" to "lament" is essential if suffering and oppressed people are to rise in protest and dignity. Her point is a valid one, and this lament and protest are often present in the religions of the oppressed before outsiders recognize them as such. The songs and prayers of people all over the world are, like the spirituals and blues of black Americans that James Cone analyzed, filled with sighs and complaints. The same is true of the poetry of Adrienne Rich, the songs of Bob Marley and the other Caribbean Rastafarians, the Ghost Dance of the Native Americans, and those various Messianic uprisings against Western colonial rule documented by Michael Adas in *Prophets of Rebellion*. These and other examples prove it is naive and historically inaccurate for revolutionary theorists always to see religion merely as opiate. The disparaging of the religions of the oppressed as pipe dreams or illusions is often done by middle-class intellectuals whose personal histories do not equip them to appreciate the crucial role the religions of poor people have played in undergirding psychic and physical survival during periods when cultural genocide and social domination were all the world seemed to offer.

What can be said about the dances, processions, and ecstatic utterances through which people voice their joy and aspiration? Such religious expressions constitute, to use Marx's other phrase, "the heart of a heartless world." They permit otherwise deprived people to share symbolically in whatever rewards can be wrested from even the most oppressive situation, and this sharing can in turn help them to discover a solidarity that provides the basis for action. A sigh is a cry, but the heart leaps up in hope. Are we reading too much into Marx's metaphors?

I think not. It is always wrong to impose a doctrine on the facts. It is mistaken to view all religion as oppressive without first examining the actual function it performs in the real lives of human beings in concrete situations. The questions must be, What do these religious practices reveal about the underlying pain, anger, alienation, and aspiration of those who thus express themselves? What ideas and values do they sanctify? One must first listen for the human through the religious and then go on to the more properly "critical" task. The Venezuelan sociologist Otto Maduro provides a good example of a scholar who uses Marxist tools but does not allow ideology to obscure reality. In his book *Religion and Social Conflict,* Otto argues, from his close observation of Latin America, that the class consciousness of an exploited people may in some situations *depend* on religion for its actual embodiment. This happens, he says, because dominated peoples experience their powerlessness in the face of what appear to be opaque and obscure forces. Therefore, religion becomes not so much a form of ideological thought as what he calls a kind of "practical ideation." Consequently, he says, for Marxists to be dogmatically atheistic, instead of focusing on the actual human and political significance of religion in such a case, can be objectively antirevolutionary, whatever its conscious intention. Otto believes that there is a contradiction between religion and atheism. But from his own Christian perspective he believes there is an even deeper contradiction between repression (whether religious or antireligious) and liberation (whether religious or antireligious).

What does it mean for theologians to make use of Marxist categories such as class, material substructure, center and periphery, and so on, in their critical analysis of religion? We reject Marxism as a dogma or as a formula for arriving at answers to difficult theological and historical issues without examining the actual case at hand. We use it as a critical method within a larger and more comprehensive approach. As Norman Gottwald puts it in *The Tribes of Yahweh:* "In adopting Marx's fertile perspective for scientific research into social phenomena we are not obliged to adopt without further examination his specific projections for the future, nor are we tied to any particular socio-political program described as Marxian."

Also, since Marx did not investigate many actual instances of religious movements, restricting himself largely to modern European ones, the use of his method does not commit us to any metaphysical faith or speculative vision about the future of religion as such. How can it then be useful? I have found it helpful in dealing with this question to recall another self-styled atheist's approach to religion, namely that of Sigmund Freud.

I want to refer here not to Freud's writings on religion as such but rather to his much more sophisticated and useful theories on the interpretation of dreams. The obvious connection between Freud and Marx is that both dreams and religious symbols express, often in coded form, the deepest layers of psychic reality. Freud once said that dreams are the "royal road to the unconscious," that is, the most effective key to the innermost strata of an individual's life. Notice however that Freudian psychoanalysis does not call for the abolition of dreams. It does not dismiss them as opiate. Rather, it is directed toward helping people to understand, maybe even to enjoy, their dreams and to become clearer about the fears and impulses expressed in them. Psychoanalysis pays attention to people's dreams in order to help them live decisively and freely because they have learned to understand these primitive drives and primal terrors and to do something about them. The objective of therapy is not to make the person stop dreaming but to discern the realities expressed in the symbolic form of dreams.

Analogously, just as psychoanalysis helps us decode dreams, an imaginitive theology can help us decode religion. If dreams are the "royal road to the unconscious" of the individual, religion can be interpreted as the royal road to the deepest corporate images of a whole people. Also, just as psychoanalytic therapy does not abolish dreaming but helps the person face the real problems that express themselves in dreams, a thoughtful theology does not try to eliminate religion but rather directs its attention to the roots of the suffering and the grounds for hope that express themselves in religion. The German Marxist Ernst Bloch argued for years that the most important function of religion is precisely its utopian dreaming, its power to provide people with an alternative: the vision of another world. Understood in this way, religion, like dreaming, can be seen as an indispensable human phenomenon. But what would be the theological equivalent for religion of the therapeutic approach to dreaming?

Faced with a world churning with upsurges of religion, what we need is a theological method that draws on the biblical revelation but is sympathetically critical of the myths, symbols, songs, prayers, and beliefs of all human beings. This critical theology would examine all these for clues to the causes of the suffering and the forces that frustrate the hopes of dominated peoples, whatever form that oppression takes. The "sigh of the oppressed creature" may be caused by poverty, alienation, ennui, powerlessness, dependency, loss of meaning, or what feminists have aptly described as "mythic oppression." Human beings still retain the capacity to cry out, to protest, to lament, to celebrate moments of release and hope. Religion is often the way they do it and is thus "the heart of a heartless world," an upsurge of feeling and defiance in a situation that punishes both.

The task of critical theology is *not* to remove the heart but to help make the world itself less heartless and not as devoid of compassion, friendship, joy, and the capacity to feel intensely. This type of theology cannot avoid being political. It will focus inevitably on those economic and social structures that cause the human distress and therefore require the utopian hoping, both of which are vented in religious expression.

Jesus and the prophets had their own sharp critique of religion. Following them, Christians can accept much of Marx's analysis of how destructively religion often functions in a "fallen world." But the Bible also presents a vision of what the world *can* be. In that biblical perspective, we can even look toward a day when there will be no need for "religion" because the heart and spirit of the world itself will have been restored. This is what the imagery of the Bible suggests when it speaks of a time when there will be "no Temple" because God will be all in all (Revelation) and no need to teach Torah because all people will already have it in their hearts (Jeremiah). The vision of the prophets is not an abolition of the sighing of oppressed creatures but the abolition of the oppression that makes the creatures sigh.

To make use of the insights of a Marxist critique of religion, Christian theologians need to develop a much more sophisticated understanding of the religion of ordinary people. This theological critique of "popular religion" is an important facet of Latin American theology, as can be seen in the work of, among others, Diego Irrarazával and Pablo Richard. In North America, however, it is still sadly underdeveloped. The historical, critical, and exegetical methods still reign supreme. Even where some attention has been paid to popular religion on this continent, it has usually been to the religion of black and other oppressed groups, to the ideological conservatism of mainline churches, or to the religious bases of male chauvinism. Here, I would like to broaden this focus and illustrate the method I have been describing by applying it to a movement I have been observing for several years, namely, neo-Oriental spirituality in the United States.

The "turning East" that I have discussed elsewhere has taken place almost entirely among white middle-class young adults, a group many liberation theologians do not find either interesting or significant. I believe, however, that an analysis of the popular religion (some form of neo-Orientalism) of these young adults reveals something significant, not just about them but about the whole society. It uncovers a pattern of dislocation and alienation among a group of financially comfortable people one might ordinarily expect to find uncritically integrated into the culture. Instead, many of them feel marginated and restless, dissatisfied with what life seems to be offering them. Why? When asked, they say that the career patterns and life-styles of the world of work and profession appear incapable of satisfying some of their most deeply felt needs. My question then is, Who are the people who are drawn into such movements? And what does their collective "sigh" tell us about at least one facet of the "heartlessness" that threatens our whole society?

First, who are they? They are certainly not the most visibly exploited people in America. Nonetheless, they are, in their own way, the victims of a painful overload of contradictions between the stated Christian and universalist value system of the society, on the one hand, and its actual capitalist utilitarian modus operandi, on the other. They are pulled apart. In family and religious life they have been taught to share and cooperate and even to love, but the world of classroom and job market requires them to connive and compete if they want to succeed. They have learned the Western emphasis on the importance of selfhood and personal experience but then find it contradicted by the discovery that one's body and mind carry a price and must be marketed. Their human developmental need to test themselves in situations of self-sacrifice and physical and mental discipline is canceled out by the ever expanding market's tendency to enlarge sales by encouraging immediate gratification, self-indulgence, and comfort. Further, the young people who join new religious groups are nearly always between their parental family and their own family and have not yet entered a career. Thus, they are temporarily outside the two major devices society uses to keep them on the tracks. The rites, beliefs, and organizational forms of the religious groups they move into represent the "sigh" of one group of "oppressed creatures" whose pain is usually not recognized when oppression is seen exclusively in economic terms but whose dilemma was clearly foreseen by Marx.

My investigations and those of my students reveal that the young people who join such movements as Hare Krishna, the Divine Light Mission, or some Buddhist and neo-Hindu groups, for example, are seeking three things. First, they are looking for a familial, affective setting instead of the fratricidal ethos of the job market. Second, they are looking for direct and unmediated experiences as opposed to the plastic, abstract world of commodities. Third, they are looking for a chance to test and stretch themselves as opposed to the debilitating pursuit of comfort that is the chief characteristic of consumer culture.

The Marxist critique can help us understand that such young people are not simply rebels without a cause. Their revolt against competition and consumerism is a revolt against some of the effects of late capitalism as these effects are felt by their particular age cohort and economic stratum. Marx believed that the profit system sets people against each other and cannot permit real fraternity or sorority to develop and that capitalism must transform objects and persons into commodities, for example, objects defined by their exchange rather than their use value, and thus make everything abstract and not susceptible to genuine human experience. He also taught that capitalism must expand its markets and thus stimulate consumerism and the cults of comfort and convenience, thereby inadvertently stimulating a hunger for discipline, simplicity, even the planned hardships that the rigors of many of the new religious movements supply.

The wave of new religious movements in the United States does not encompass large numbers of people. Does it tell us something about the culture as a whole? I believe it can. It can be seen as an unconscious and prepolitical rejection of the dehumanizing results of consumer capitalism, at least of its results in one sector of the population. Notice it is a revolt against the *results* of the profit-consumer system, not against the system itself; consequently, middle-class political thinkers of a leftist orientation often look at these movements as regressive. Ironically, status quo conservatives also see them as a threat since the new movements sometimes encourage young people to abandon conventional career goals and consumerist life-styles (to drop out of law school or eat tofu). Significantly, however, the rituals and belief systems of these groups often reinforce attitudes of nondependency on the established economic structures, values, and life patterns. Adherents often do not consume new dress styles, rely far less on mass media for signals, reject the merchandising pseudo-eroticism of advertising, and sometimes prefer to educate their own children rather than sending them to either elite private schools or public schools. They often support themselves financially by organizing their own small-scale cooperative businesses rather than working for large corporations. Significantly, they avoid psychotherapy because they are suspicious of its adjustment orientation.

What do these movements tell us about America? I believe the new religious movements in the United States represent a crack in the commodity-consumer cultural fortress. They are vulnerable, of course, both to co-optation and to control by the powers that be, but that is all the more reason why they should not be dismissed as a diversion or a mere mystification. People who are looking for some alternative are at least one step ahead of those who remain dumb and mute. The wave of participation in such movements reveals "the heart of a heartless world" and expresses the sigh of creatures who are not yet completely aware of the real sources of their discomfort.

What I have said so far will indicate how my use of some elements of Marxism has carried me beyond my book *Turning East*. But I also believe this approach could be broadened to include other theological and religious considerations, including our current concern for interreligious dialogue. Our task is first of all to understand the human significance of religion in particular cases and then to move, as Marx says, "from criticism of heaven to the criticism of earth." I am suggesting that a new type of theology is emerging, one that could be described as "inductive" rather than "deductive," one that listens to the voices of the people and tries to help them relate God to their own human "logos." Here again the analogy of the therapist helps: the theologian should help people become more aware so they can act more decisively.

Any theology, including a theology sharpened by the tools of a Marxist critique of religion, should produce a form of pastoral practice. To develop such a practice, we must begin by recognizing that both Christians and members of other faith traditions have introjected ideas of God imposed on them by the religious ideology of dominating groups. Therefore they experience God as a wholly external power on whom one must depend for survival. But pastoral practice depends on the fact that this internalization of the dominant religious ideology is never complete. There is always a core of real experience that can be called on. Just as psychoanalytic treatment uses this core to help a person reclaim projected and alienated parts of oneself into one's own person, so theology should help peoples reclaim powers of their own that are now invested in external objects. In biblical language, the proclamation of the Word awakens people to the recognition that God has already come to them and become a partner in their struggles: "He who was once far off has drawn near" and is the one who inspires, supports, nourishes and also suffers with anyone who is oppressed. But just as therapists cannot merely deliver this message but must help their clients experience it in their own terms, so theologians cannot merely deliver their ideas but must watch, listen, feel, and help people make the connection in their own world of religious imagery.

The foregoing exposition suggests to me that, in order to develop such a pastoral practice in the United States, we still need a dialogue between Christian theology and certain elements of Marxist social analysis. In recent years, after promising beginnings in Europe, the interaction of Christians and Marxists turned to discussions about imperialism, neocolonialism, and other issues felt mainly in the Third World. Ironically, this has led North American and Western European Christians to the belief that, although a Marxist analysis might be applicable in faraway places or to relations between the central and peripheral countries, it is irrelevant at home.

Some writers even suggested that the only thing concerned North Americans and Europeans could do was to live in solidarity with Third World revolutions. Ironically, rebels like Che Guevarra became romantic heroes to young people who were unaware of or unwilling to recognize the potential for change in their own lands. This fascination with distant revolutions is also a kind of alienation. It caused many young people—mainly in the white middle class—to ignore the possible relevance of Marxist analysis to the contradictions in their own lives and the ills of their own society.

We need to remind ourselves that the critique of imperialism is only a part of Marxist thought. By focusing entirely on imperialism, North Americans often forgot their own situation. Marx not only criticized capitalism for its failure to provide distributive justice—he also criticized it for destroying the work experience itself by fragmenting, alienating, and abstracting it, therefore distorting its essential human quality. This is a crucial point since, although most Americans can identify with the Third World struggle only in a limited way, they taste the boredom every time they sit down at the computer terminal. Marxist analysis thus applies just as much to North American society itself as it does to the relationship between North American corporations and the countries that have been made dependent on them. In fact, these two phases of the analysis must go together if either is to be persuasive. I see the new religious movements in the United States as symptoms of a more pervasive dislocation, as expressions of protest and lament, as efforts—unsuccessful so far—to find some alternative to the consumerist life.

A critical pastoral practice in America requires us to understand those dislocations in our society that result in the competitiveness that destroys friendship, the commodity fetishism that makes all experience seem vaguely unreal, and the consumerism that makes idols out of comfort and convenience. I do not believe that we will take even one step toward a North American theology of liberation until we grow away from a romantic identification with guerillas in the South American hills and look instead at the sources of our own discontent. This discontent is not only the suffering of the poor and the old. It also extends to those who in work and family life feel—as Marx said they would—the awful tyranny of the bottom line.

Ironically, some of the great atheist's ideas might end up helping people who have taken the first, confused steps against the values of consumer-competitive culture go deeper. Such people are looking for friends in small religious groupings, but what we need is a whole society in which fraternity is possible. Otherwise human existence will remain schizophrenic. By practicing yoga and meditation, they seek to reclaim both their minds and their bodies from being distorted into commodities. What is needed is a world that does not rob us of our own bodies and our work by transforming them into items for sale. They seek to escape the debilitating effect of consumer comforts by accepting the arduous disciplines of messiahs and meditation masters. What is needed is an economy in which cooperation and service are rewarded rather than punished. As we begin to look below the surface of the new middle-class religious movements and see them as sighs of oppression and cries of protest, we will be led to a more constructive pastoral approach to them, and we will find that a common enemy, the spirit of profit at all costs, robs all of us of our God-given humanity.

9

The Future of Religion

When all is said and done, is there anything we can confidently predict about the future of religion? Why not hazard a few guesses? After all, past predictions about other forms of human endeavor have often been borne out. Observe: we do have space ships, death rays, annihilation weapons, and happy pills, just as Jules Verne and Aldous Huxley once imagined. But religion is notoriously harder to predict. What Nostradamus could have foreseen the resurgence of militant Islam, a tongue-speaking charismatic revival among middle-class Americans, a Korean evangelist resurrecting the old American civil religion with himself as the presumptive messiah? Or a twentieth-century pope who poses for photographs with a sombrero on, like an American presidential candidate? Or the reemergence of witchcraft? In taking on this most perilous of all fields of forecast, it might be useful to recall three of the more notable past predictions, all of which seem to have come to nought.

The Philosophes

Let us begin with a distinguished company: the eighteenth-century French philosophes. Since they believed the Age of Reason was dawning, the philosophes confidently predicted that religion and superstition were fated for extinction, presumably quite soon. Their *Encyclopedia* was to be a compendium of all knowledge, shining the bright light of human intelligence into the darkest abyss, expelling the noisome remains of priestcraft and sorcery. Religion, they believed, was the product of ignorance compounded by clerical greed and political reaction. It was a poison whose only antidote was clear and courageous thought. "Not until the last priest is hanged with the entrails of the last king," Voltaire once declared, "will mankind finally be free." So they enthroned the goddess Reason, carried her in solemn procession through Paris, accompanied by young girls strewing flowers, bore her into Notre Dame Cathedral, hymned her virtues, and dedicated the dawning new age to her.

How were they to know that with procession, enthroning, and hymning they were perpetuating religion, not abolishing it? Human beings have made the same mistake before and since. Auguste Comte, the founder of positivism, was in some ways the last of the philosophes. He thought he saw humankind leaving behind mythical and metaphysical explanations of reality and entering the "positive" age. In fact, he became so enchanted with his vision that he went on to compose a whole Mass for the era of positivism. It is a curious and wonderful artifice, this Mass, containing all the traditional pillars of the Roman original but reworked for a positivist Weltanschauung. Religion seems to reassert itself even among those who most avidly desire its demise. The predictions of the philosophes seem not to have come true, even for them.

Lenin and Marx

Lenin is another case in point. With a mind somewhat more programmatic and less flexible than Marx's, he took quite woodenly his master's ideas about religion and enlarged them into a metaphysical worldview he believed would soon replace religion. Lenin utilized some of the evolutionist and physical materialist ideas then prevalent to produce his own theory of materialism, one which was, however, ontological, not dialectical like Marx's. Lenin's concoction, although popular with Russian Communists for many years, is rarely defended nowadays. Most Marxists prefer to follow Marx instead of Lenin and to make their judgments about religion on a political, rather than an ontological, basis. Ironically, a half century after the October revolution, not only has religion not died out in Lenin's Soviet Union, but the most widely appreciated Russian writers, Aleksandr Solzhenitsyn and Andrei Sinyavsky, are Orthodox believers, as was the late Boris Pasternak. Whatever else his accomplishments, as a religious forecaster Lenin, like the philosophes, seems to have failed.

Lenin's predictions were confounded by his own fate. When this enemy of all pilgrimages and icons and superstitious devotions died, his body was embalmed and placed in a mausoleum in Red Square in the shadow of Saint Basil's. There, to this day, thousands of pilgrims wend their way, lining up in every kind of weather to file past the sacred bier. The lights are dim in the tomb of Lenin. An atmosphere of sanctity and hushed awe pervades the stone temple. Some older pilgrims from the far provinces are seen to cross themselves as they shuffle by the glass-encased remains of the saint. And behold, as young Alexis Karamazov had vainly hoped for *his* idol, Father Zossima, the body remains uncorrupted—the result this time not of a miracle but of the embalming techniques of modern science. The enemy of icons has been made into an icon himself.

Freud and Jung

Let us look at one more prediction before—duly humbled by these discouraging precedents—we venture a few of our own. No catalog of "past futures" of religion would be complete without that of Sigmund Freud, whose *Future of an Illusion* represents his most concisely worded entry into this precarious enterprise. Freud believed that religion consisted of the projection of inner fears and anxieties—and hopes and fantasies—onto the external world. He interpreted it as a kind of infantile delusion writ large. As the inventor of psychoanalysis, he had strong confidence in the efficacy of his method. He saw it as the ultimate application of the scientific method—which had formerly scanned the skies—to the inner, secret workings of the human mind. He hoped that eventually the utilization of this method would enable people to set aside religious delusions and face reality without blinders and crutches.

But Freud did not seem to believe this psychoanalytic remedy would take effect very quickly or even in the foreseeable future. The illusion was too widespread and too well grounded in the culture itself. In fact, there are passages in which Freud appears to have resigned himself to a kind of pessimism, in which he seems to be saying that, since his solution will never be generalizable to the whole populace, the "illusion" may have a promising future indeed.

Freud's body was never enshrined in a holy sepulcher, as Lenin's was. But before his death, as though to prove once again the futility of making predictions about the fate of the gods, Freud's criticism of religion was turned inside out by one of his own disciples, Carl Gustaf Jung. His thought may be for Freud what the Red Square tomb became for Lenin.

The son of a Swiss Reformed pastor, as a child Jung once had a dream in which an immense divinity squatted in the sky over the local cathedral and defecated on its soaring tower. Although this does not appear to be the dream of a man who would later start from Freud's thinking and then move toward a whole new rationale for the religious understanding of life, that is in fact exactly what Jung did. His theories, and the form of therapy associated with his name, have conspired to produce an attitude toward religion for numerous twentieth-century people who can no longer be religious in conventional ways. Like Freud, the Jungians see the whole pantheon of the gods as an internal universe, not something "out there." But in contrast to Freud, they believe these gods are not to be abolished, outgrown, unmasked, or eviscerated. Rather, one should learn to know them and serve them, for in so doing one is serving one's own deepest and most authentic self.

At this point, any sensible student of the history and philosophy of religion would stop. Having demonstrated the precariousness of extrapolations in the realm of the spirit, the best expression of wisdom would be a Buddha-like smile—and silence. It was Jesus himself who said, "The spirit bloweth where it listeth, and no man knows from whence it comes or whither it blows." (He also held in singularly low regard those who thought they could predict "the day or the hour of the coming of the Son of Man," a secret that, he said, was known only to the Father in heaven.) In short, all evidence, both historical and theological, seems to point to a strategy of restraint, abjuring all predictions. But who—despite the cautionary tales of past failures—can resist making at least some attempt to predict something about the future of religion? I will ignore the evidence and plunge ahead.

After this dismal recitation of failed fathers, I still contend that all three of the predictions I have just cataloged about the future of religion—those of the philosophes, of Marx, and of Freud—though flawed in detail, have turned out to be *essentially* accurate. In one sense, they all seem to have missed, but I believe they each teach us something valid, or at least useful.

Let us look at them once again, in order. First, the philosophes. They were correct, in my view, to foresee the disappearance of religion as an extension of that way of knowing the external world we now call magic or superstition. Religion is not the descendant of magic. The magical impulse is the desire to control and direct nature, to use it for human ends, to tame its sometimes malevolent side. This impulse developed through the centuries not into religion but into empirical science. The true successors of the sorcerers and the alchemists are not the priests and theologians but the physicists and the computer engineers. They merely use another method to accomplish the same end. Religion has nothing to do with supplying answers to questions that can be answered by empirical investigation and observation. Religion concerns questions of human meaning and purpose that are in principle unanswerable in an empirical way. (This holds unless one believes that ethical imperatives and human meaning can simply be deduced from how things are, a questionable theory that cannot itself be proven by observing how things are.)

In other words, the notorious nineteenth-century "Warfare between Science and Religion" arose from mistaken notions of what religion and science are. Although there are still occasional border skirmishes, most theologians and scientists now recognize that religion overstepped its boundaries when—at least in the West—it tried to make geological and biological history into matters of revelation. On the other side, although some scientists once believed they had discovered the universal method for solving all conceivable questions—rather than one very useful way of dealing with some—it is very hard to get an argument going between scientists and theologians over issues of this kind any more. At the international conference on "Science, Faith and the Future" sponsored by the World Council of Churches at the Massachusetts Institute of Technology in July 1979, there was virtually no debate along the old science-versus-religion lines at all. Rather, the scientists implored the theologians and religious leaders present to take more of an interest in the pressing ethical issues emerging from the newest advances of science. Theologians, especially from the poorer parts of the world, did not criticize the scientists for being too self-important. Rather, they took them to task for making big hardware for the multinational corporations instead of supplying appropriate technologies to the poorer countries. The issues, in other words, were political and ethical, and it was clear that the deepest divisions pitted North against South, rich against poor, East against West, radical against liberal.

As it turns out, the philosophes' attack on religion had a kind of purgative effect. More and more, religion is now concerning itself with questions of human meaning and ethical policy, not with dogmatic formulations about what time of day it was when God created the world (a question that had vexed the nineteenth-century British Anglican Bishop Ussher).

Even in Iran, where a form of Muslim zealotry has reemerged, it is significant to notice that the ayatollahs and imams have not attacked the domain of science as such but have concentrated on what they see as issues of public order. The direction the philosophes set out is still, when its exaggerations are combed out, what we too can expect in the future: realizing its limitations, we will turn to science for help in answering the how and why questions. At the same time the perennial riddles of human meaning and personal obligation will continue to be debated in categories derived from the great religious traditions.

How else could it be? The most important questions we will face in the future must be answered on the basis of premises about the nature and destiny of humankind for which no empirical proof can be mustered. What is human life, and when does it begin or end? Is every human life really worth respecting? If so, why? Has the present generation any responsibility for those who will inherit the planet millennia from now? Does the human species have any special responsibility at all in the cosmos? Is there a meaning that transcends my meaning or even the collective total of all our human meanings? Is there anything worth dying for? All these questions press the questioner ultimately into those strata of human reality where our primal terrors and hopes—expressed in myth and rite and symbol—remain the only sources of wisdom.

But what about Marxism? Surely Lenin's idea that religious life can be reduced to emanations from material particles that are then used to justify class oppression in no way depicts the future of religion. Again, let us step back from the precise manner in which Lenin (and Marx, in a much more subtle way) actually enunciated their theories and look instead at the overall intention of their program. Although Lenin's metaphysical views are dated ones and now appear positively quaint, there are three aspects of his and of Marx's ideas about religion that I consider basically sound.

First, they insisted that religion must be understood not in isolation but in relation to all other dimensions of life, including the way human beings use the natural world to feed and clothe themselves. Religion, they believed—and quite rightly—does not fall like fire from the heavens. It is part and parcel with all other human activities and cannot be fathomed without reference to them. Lenin called his way of analyzing this totality "materialistic" because of his neo-Democritean (from Democritus, the Greek atomic materialist) ontology. Marx preferred the term "dialectical." What they both wanted to say is that the study of "religion" *as such* can teach us nothing. We must study it as an integral element of the world of work and power and social arrangements. In this, they were right. More and more I am suspicious of that method of studying religion represented by Joseph Campbell and Mircea Eliade. The typical approach of these highly influential scholars is to assemble the myths and legends of several cultures into a collection in a skillful way but with few descriptions of the social settings within which actual people told, sang, chanted, or danced the myths. They are set down in print, often thematically organized. Tribes and continents are juxtaposed with very little indication of who tells them and who listens, how the tribe feeds itself or is governed, to say nothing of what happens to the people—if there are any—who don't like the story. In short, the error of this widespread method is that it lifts out something called "religion" from the intricate human corpus in which it lives. The result is a kind of collage of disparate elements that disfigures the religious dimensions. For all their understandable nineteenth-century philosophical narrowness, Marx and Lenin did not want this kind of excising to happen, and in this they were right.

Second, Marx and his followers saw that, in an unjust society, religion is a powerful tool of oppression. It is an opiate, a mystification, a way of trying to solve through fantasy what can be solved only in history. Again, although they were undoubtedly heavy-handed in the way they laid out this criticism, no one can doubt that they were largely correct, at least for the societies in which they lived. During the nineteenth-century, religious institutions played an almost exclusively reactionary role nearly everywhere. Marx and his followers took deadly aim; they pointed out that, since religion is part of a sociocultural whole and culture is almost always controlled by the dominant group, religion can be a tool of manipulation. This leaves us to wonder what religion might look like in a nonexploitative society, where there would be no need for opiates to keep people subdued and mystified. I will return to this point later.

Third, Marx and his school believed that religion would eventually disappear. Again, though this may come as a surprise to the reader, I believe they were right. Marx's notion about the "disappearance" of religion can be understood best by comparing it with his theory about the "withering away of the state." This idea has also been roundly ridiculed, largely because it is so badly misunderstood. What he meant was that there is nothing eternally fixed about any human institution, the state included. It is a perfectly reasonable idea when one thinks about it for a moment. For millennia, human societies existed and governed themselves before the institution of the state appeared. National states emerged at a certain point in recent history, served and will serve a certain purpose, but will not endure forever. As awareness expands and new forms of consciousness and culture evolve, new patterns of governance, which are not as distant and hard to control as the state, will also appear, Marx thought.

The comparison with religion is quite exact. Just as something called the "state" differentiated itself from that great complex organism we now call "society" at one stage in its history, so we also began to speak of certain acts and persons and institutions as "religious." But this is a very recent category of human thought and I believe also a "reified" one. The Balinese, it is said, claim they have no art: they just do everything beautifully. There was a time, not too long ago in the full scale of cultural evolution, when one would have been hard put to discover anything separate and distinct in human societies that could be called "religion." People just "did everything" with awe or joy or with a sense of mystery or with a recognition of the incandescent power within persons, places, and things. Prayer was as much a part of planting as invocation was of hunting. It is possible that, in our efforts to understand the cultures of the Orient and of nonliterate peoples, much mischief and confusion has already resulted from our imposing on them the—Western and recent—term "religion." What Marx meant, perhaps, is that we now live in an unnatural epoch, one in which we have separated and elevated (and mystified) something we call "religion." Eventually, when conditions allow for the transition, this artificially segregated element will be reabsorbed into the whole.

Finally, what about Freud, Jung, and the psychological predictions about religion? Although religious scholars often prefer Jung since he is notoriously "soft" on myth, magic, and astrology, I prefer Freud. The old master of the Bergstrasse was right that much of religion consists of the projection of inner fantasies onto an imaginary external screen. Unlike Jung, Freud did not want to come to terms with this projecting, but he could not see how we could get beyond it either. He chose to live with the tension, and his choice has given rise to two remarkably differing interpretations of what the next step after his own work should have been. Some sought to help people do the best they can in a world in which some degree of neurotic projection will inevitably continue even after it is minimized in individual patients. Most practicing therapists settle for this interpretation of the master. The other side will not accept this compromise. The "radical Freudians" claim that there is implicit in Freud the idea that we should alter the conditions that produce this "surplus repression" with its resultant neurosis. If we did, alienated human thinking and living would be transcended, not by treating two billion people one by one for four years each at seventy-five dollars an hour, but by a quantum leap in human awareness, growing out of a qualitative change in the basic organization of human life. If this great leap could happen, then the present, unconscious inclination to segregate religious impulses from the rest of life would slip into the past, and we would deal with the universe, our neighbors, and ourselves without the mediation of mystified phantoms.

This vision of the radical Freudians, represented most eloquently in the thought of the late Herbert Marcuse, admittedly sounds terribly utopian, maybe even "millenarian." It is at least—to use a very theological term—"eschatological." It suggests a Messianic Era or a Kingdom of God. Freud remained stalwartly antireligious to his dying day. But the logic of his thought, at least as it is interpreted by his radical disciples, conjures up images similar to that of the prophet Jeremiah, who spoke of a coming time when no one would have to speak the name of God or teach the law since God would be within us and the law would be inscribed on our hearts. The New Testament book of Revelation tells of a heavenly city where there is no need for a temple because God suffuses everything. Ironically, the radical Freudians are closer to the Bible than the pious Jungians.

True, one could argue that all the predictions I have mentioned were wrong. Despite the *Encyclopedia,* religion has not disappeared. Despite Marx and Lenin, there is a religious revival going on in Eastern Europe and the USSR, and in Latin America the Catholics are more revolutionary than the Communists. Fifty years after Freud's death, psychoanalysis is dying. Still, each of these prophets had a point. The philosophes' forecasts remind us that religion should not be mistaken for a method of examining and managing empirical reality. Marx and Lenin are right that religion is part and parcel with the whole of the human world, and its use for exalted and debased purposes cannot be understood if it is studied in isolation. They also teach us that religion is not simply a part of "nature," given once and for all, but a part of "history" and therefore subject to conscious criticism and reconstruction. Finally, the Freudians remind us that even if religion springs from deep and possibly distorted needs in the human psyche, its inner logic points to the possibility of a fundamentally different kind of world order.

Where does all this leave us? It seems appropriate to conclude our reflections on the future of religion with a parable, this one the true story of one American congregation. During the War for Independence, there were many patriots in the new nation who thought that a new day had come in religion also. They were sure they were the midwives for this new religion, which they intended to deliver, not just to America, but to the world. The case of King's Chapel in Boston serves as a particularly good example. It had been, in the period before independence, an Anglican chapel serving the needs of the small community that still adhered to the Church of England in that Puritan theocratic outpost. When the war began, the position of theological and political loyalists became a bit less secure than the rock of ages. Eventually, when the British troops themselves evacuated Boston, King's Chapel suffered the hasty departure of its rector and many of its more Tory-minded parishioners.

The remnant was left in an unusually precarious but promising position. In fact, their canonical situation was virtually unique. Since the king of England, who had headed the Anglican church since Henry VIII, no longer ruled this realm, their ties with the Anglican hierarchy were severed with one hurried sailing. Also, since they had never been subject to the Standing Order—the established Puritan-Calvinist church of the Massachusetts Bay Colony—they now found themselves, in effect, the freest church in Boston. But what should that freedom mean?

A long discussion ensued about what a truly "republican religion" should be. Would it be deist, evangelical, unitarian? In one sense, the congregation of King's Chapel undertook the same task the French philosophes had accomplished by creating the goddess Reason. But unlike them, or Marx and Lenin, who saw no need for any religion, they wanted to formulate a religious doctrine that would be patriotic, enlightened, and in keeping with that special destiny many Americans believed "nature's God" intended for the new republic. The argument raged on, and the mixture of religious theories and political posturing that appeared was heady stuff indeed. The result, as might have been expected, was a fascinating compromise that any visitor to Boston can still sample by stopping in at King's Chapel. The "republican religion" for the new nation turned out to be an admixture of unitarian theology and Anglican liturgical forms. The church now belongs to the Unitarian-Universalist denomination, but the shape of its liturgy is "higher" than even that of many American Episcopal churches. In few other places can parishioners actually chant liberal theological paeans in something close to Gregorian plainsong.

To the question of whether the congregants of King's Chapel actually anticipated the religion of the future or even the religion of the new republic, one can offer only an inconclusive answer at best. True, their deliberations produced what harsher critics might call a potpourri of ingredients whose proportions did not catch on with the rest of the population of the new nation. Still, the important thing is that they made the attempt. Some political historians argue that it was not until the English revolution of the seventeenth century that people began to realize that the forms of governance they had simply taken for granted as being "natural"—the monarchy, for example—were not "natural" at all but were products of human construction in history and could therefore be altered or abolished. The people of King's Chapel were merely applying this same principle to religious life. They were taking what had once been viewed as a "given" into their own hands and consciously shaping it for human ends. They were "defatalizing" their religious lives just as they were also applying the human tendency to reshape, remold, and reform in other realms. They teach us something important about the future of religion not by what they did but by the courage and initiative they showed in daring to do it. We now have the chance to do the same thing—not to wait and see what religious forms will emerge in the next century, but to use our imaginations to shape them.

So what then about the future of religion? Personally, I believe those kinds of questions we currently segregate and call "religion" will not disappear so long as there are people around to ask them. Human beings come into life without having asked for it. They inherit a skin and sex and culture they never chose. They are buffeted with pain, lifted with joys, strangled by deprivation, awed by the inevitability of death. They are enraged by injustice and dream of a better way. Human beings always spawn more questions than they can answer. If they could only be *either* goats or gods instead of this curious combination, there would be no "religion." Still, as long as there is something recognizably human to hope for and ponder and question, there will be the "religious dimension." But will it always have the strangely segregated and fenced-off place it now seems so "naturally" to occupy in our epoch?

I doubt it. Students of Chinese history have often remarked on the way the sacred seems to be imbedded in the everyday. One writer calls Taoism "the sacrality of the secular." But does this mean the Chinese are "less religious"? Or more so? Perhaps future historians will look back on our modern Western age as an aberration, one in which the spiritual ingredient of life was distilled, drawn off, encapsulated—with disastrous results.

I do not believe my future vision of a religion reintegrated into the secular conflicts with Christianity. Dietrich Bonhoeffer, the German pastor who wrote his *Letters and Papers From Prison* while awaiting his execution by the Nazis, once said he never really wanted to become a saint; he just wanted "to be a man." To be a Christian, he said, was, in the final analysis, to be fully human. He rejected any "magic helper" notion of God and insisted that God had become a partner in the earthly reality, sharing our weakness, eliciting our strength. He even talked about the need for a "non-religious interpretation of the Gospel," but he was hanged by the Gestapo before he could begin to work out his ideas.

Bonhoeffer died in the spring of 1945, just hours before the advancing American forces reached the concentration camp where he was incarcerated. A few months later a plane named the Enola Gay flew over the city of Hiroshima and dropped the first atomic bomb. These two events, taken together, symbolize something unprecedented about the questions human beings ask about themselves and their futures, including the future of religion. In the last weeks of his life, Bonhoeffer glimpsed a new world emerging in which Christianity would assume a shape so radically different that he predicted it would be virtually unrecognizable to his contemporaries. The dropping of the atomic bomb, however, wrote a mushroom-shaped question mark after any and all speculations about the human future. It has also radically altered the question of the future of religion.

In his essay "The Mysticism of Science," Pierre Teilhard de Chardin, one of the most influential Catholic thinkers of our time, remarked that the two essential ingredients of any religion are "hope and the vista of a limitless future." In this short phrase he has put his finger exactly on the only authentically "religious" question of the post-Hiroshima era. Stated in its simplest form, our religious concern about the future must not be about the "future of religion" but about the future per se. Any "religious hope" today must begin with the hope that there will in fact be a human future. Such a hope must be "religious" because the empirical basis for it is ambiguous at best. Since Hiroshima and the stacking up of nuclear armed rockets, the answer to the question is in no way self-evident. For the first time in human memory there is room to doubt whether our species has any future at all. Teilhard envisioned humankind as just now entering on that exciting and critical new phase of evolution—its next "nodal point," as he called it—in which, at last, the future would be in human hands. But he did not foresee The Button, which is also in human hands.

Reviewing past forecasts about the future of religion can be helpful, but only up to a point. Making predictions can be valuable, but also misleading. The great new fact of the possibility of species suicide transforms not just the context in which our question about the future of religion is voiced but the nature of the question itself. As creatures embedded in history, we cannot ask these questions from some Copernican vantage point situated outside the threats and uncertainties of terrestrial existence. To think in such an abstract way can only be an ominous symptom of our refusal to take responsibility for the real world in which we must live. "Predicting" the future subtly perpetuates the idea that someone or something else controls it, when the truth is, as both Bonhoeffer and Teilhard knew, it is now in our hands. And, as religious people would say, it is in our hands because God has placed it there. Thus, the possibility of self-annihilation requires us to put all our questions not in the form, What will happen? but rather in the form, What must we do? We cannot merely speculate on whether rites and myths will someday cease to divide and stupefy people; we must so shape and reconceive them that they unite and enlarge us. We cannot afford to wait and see whether the "religious dimension" ceases to be a segregated precinct; we must set about making it an integral dimension of all we do. We cannot allow denominations, hierarchies, and confessional strife to continue to run their course as though what happened in the "sacred realm" lay outside our human capacity to mold and steer. But we cannot, like the God of scholastic theology, create the future ex nihilo. As time-bound creatures, we must work with the stubborn stuff of past and present. Among the "givens" are our existing religious traditions, which, far from dying out, appear to be leaping into a period of resurgence. But neither can we wait for kismet to deliver us into a new era in which we no longer need to project our inmost terrors onto the heavens or onto other peoples and nations. We must now take the initiative, not just to predict the future—including the future of religion—but to shape it.

Bibliography

Adas, Michael. *Prophets of Rebellion: Millenarian Protest Movements against European Colonial Order*. Chapel Hill, N.C.: University of North Carolina Press, 1979.

Anderson, Gerald G., and Thomas F. Stransky. *Christ's Lordship and Religious Pluralism*. Maryknoll, N.Y.: Orbis Books, 1981.

Arberry, A. J., trans. *The Koran Interpreted*. New York: Macmillan, 1955.

Asman, Fathi, Zalman Schacter, Gerard Sloyan, and Dermot Lane. "Jesus in Jewish-Christian-Muslim Dialogue." *Journal of Ecumenical Studies* 14, no. 3 (Summer 1977):448ff.

Azari, Farah. *Women of Iran: The Conflict with Fundamentalist Islam*. London: Ithaca Press, 1983.

Babb, Laurence A. *The Divine Hierarchy: Popular Hinduism in Central India*. New York: Columbia University Press, 1975.

Bassuk, Daniel E. *Incarnation in Hinduism and Christianity*. Atlantic Highlands, N.J.: Humanities Press, 1987.

Buber, Martin. *A Land of Two Peoples*. Oxford: Oxford University Press, 1983.

Chogyam Trungpa. *Cutting through Spiritual Materialism*. Boston: Shambhala, 1987.

Coward, Harold. *Pluralism: Challenge to World Religions*. Maryknoll, N.Y.: Orbis Books, 1985.

Cragg, Kenneth. *The Call of the Minaret*. New York: Oxford University Press, 1964.

Cragg, Kenneth, and R. Marston Speight. *Islam from Within*. Belmont, Calif.: Wadsworth, 1980.

Dumont, Louis. *Homo Hierarchicus: The Caste System and Its Implications*. London: Paladin, 1972.

Fackenheim, Emil. *God's Presence in History*. New York: NYU Press, 1972.

Friedman, Maurice. *Martin Buber's Life and Work*. New York: E. P. Dutton, 1981.

Gill, Sam. *Beyond the "Primitive": Religions of Nonliterate Peoples*. Englewood Cliffs, N.J.: Prentice Hall, 1982.

Goitein, S. D. *From the Land of Sheba: Tales of the Jews of Yemen*. New York: Schocken Books, 1947.

———. *Jews and Arabs: Their Contacts through the Ages*. 3d edition. New York: Schocken Books, 1974.

Gregg, Kenneth. *The Call of the Minaret*. New York: Oxford University Press, 1956.

Hawley, John Stratton, and Donna Marie Wulff, eds. *The Divine Consort: Radha and the Goddesses of India*. Boston: Beacon Press, 1986.

Hay, Malcolm. *Thy Brother's Blood: The Roots of Christian Anti-Semitism*. New York: Hart, 1975.

Hick, John, and Paul Knitter, eds. *The Myth of Christian Uniqueness: Toward a Pluralistic Theology of Religions*. Maryknoll, N.Y.: Orbis Books, 1987.

Hopkins, Thomas J. *The Hindu Religious Tradition*. Belmont, Calif.: Wadsworth, 1971.

Jones, Violet Rhoda, and L. Bertan. *Woman in Islam*. Lucknow: Lucknow Publishing House, 1941.

Keddie, Nikki R. *An Islamic Response to Imperialism*. Berkeley: University of California Press, 1983.

Kingsley, David R. *The Sound of the Flute: Kali and Krsna, Dark*

Visions of the Terrible and the Sublime in Hindu Mythology. Berkeley: University of California Press, 1975.

Kline, George L. *Religious and Anti-Religious Thought in Russia*. Chicago: University of Chicago Press, 1968.

Knitter, Paul. *No Other Name? A Critical Survey of Christian Attitudes toward the World Religions*. Maryknoll, N.Y.: Orbis Books, 1985.

Küng, Hans, and Jürgen Moltmann. *Christianity among World Religions*. Concilium 1986, vol. 193. Edinburgh: T. & T. Clark, 1986.

Lewis, Bernard. *The Political Language of Islam*. Chicago: University of Chicago Press, 1988.

Lindsey, Hal, and C. C. Carlson. *The Late Great Planet Earth*. Grand Rapids, Mich.: Zondervan, 1970.

Lopez, Donald, Jr., and Steven Rockefeller, eds. *The Christ and the Bodhisattva*. Albany: SUNY Press, 1987.

Majumdar, A. K. Caitanya: *His Life and Doctrine*. Bombay: Bharatiyer Vidya Bhavan, 1969.

Marglin, Frédérique Apffel. *Wives of the God-King: The Rituals of the Devadasis of Puri*. Oxford: Oxford University Press, 1985.

Masaryk, Thomas. *The Spirit of Russia*. London and New York: Macmillan, 1955.

Memmi, Albert. *The Colonizer and the Colonized*. Boston: Beacon Press, 1967.

Metz, Johann Baptist. *The Emergent Church: The Future of Christianity in a Postbourgeois World*. New York: Crossroads, 1981.

Miliukov, Paul. *Outlines of Russian Culture, Part I: Religion and the Church*. New York: A. S. Barnes, 1960.

Mokashi, D. B. *Palkhi: An Indian Pilgrimage*. Albany: SUNY Press, 1987.

Narasimha, N. S. *The Way of Vaisnava Sages*. New York: University Press of America, 1987.

Neusner, Jacob. *Self-Fulfilling Prophecy: Exile and Return in the History of Judaism*. Boston: Beacon Press, 1987.

Obermann, Heiko. *The Roots of Anti-Semitism in the Age of the Renaissance and Reformation.* Philadelphia: Fortress Press, 1983.

O'Flaherty, Wendy. *Asceticism and Eroticism in the Mythology of Siva.* London: Oxford University Press, 1973.

Pagels, Elaine. *The Gnostic Gospels.* New York: Random House, 1979.

Panikkar, Raymond. *The Unknown Christ in Hinduism.* Revised edition. Maryknoll, N.Y.: Orbis Books, 1982.

Parshall, Phil. *Bridges to Islam: A Christian Perspective on Folk Islam.* Grand Rapids, Mich.: Baker Book House, 1983.

Pascal, Pierre. *The Religion of the Russian People.* Crestwood, N.Y.: St. Vladimir's Seminary Press, 1976.

Race, Alan. *Christians and Religious Pluralism.* Maryknoll, N.Y.: Orbis Books, 1982.

Rahula, Walpola. *What the Buddha Taught.* New York: Grove, 1959.

Roy, Manisha. *Bengali Women.* Chicago: University of Chicago Press, 1975.

Schimmel, Annemarie. *And Muhammed Is His Messenger.* Chapel Hill, N.C.: University of North Carolina Press, 1985.

Segal, Alan. *Rebecca's Children: Judaism and Christianity in the Roman World.* Cambridge, Mass.: Harvard University Press, 1986.

Sobrino, Jon. *Christology at the Crossroads: A Latin American Approach.* London: SCM Press, 1978.

Thomas, M. M. *The Acknowledged Christ of the Indian Renaissance.* London, SCM Press, 1969.

———. *Risking Christ for Christ's Sake: Towards an Ecumenical Theology of Pluralism.* Geneva: WCC Publications, 1987.

van Leeuwen, Arend T. *Christianity in World History: The Meeting of the Faiths of East and West.* London: Edinburgh House Press, 1964.

Zenovsky, V. V. *A History of Russian Philosophy.* London: Routledge & Kegan Paul, 1953.